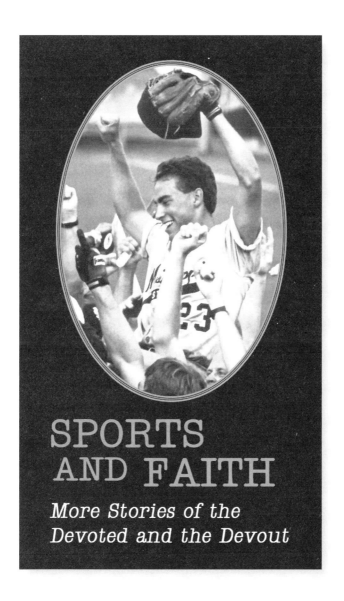

SPORTS AND FAITH

More Stories of the Devoted and the Devout

PATRICK McC...

Sporting Chance Press™, Inc.
1074 Butler Drive Crystal Lake, IL 60014
sportingchancepress.com

Ecclesiastes 3:1, Nehemiah 1:5-11, Isaiah 40:31, Luke 4:18, Philippians 3:14, Joshua 1:9, Proverbs 19:21, 2 Timothy 4:6-8, 1 Corinthians 9:24-27, Ephesians 6:10, Proverbs 31:10-31, Luke 5:32, Psalms 28:7, Hebrews 12:1-3, Joshua 24:15, Sirach 3:12-14, Philippians 4:8, 1 Timothy 4:6-8, and Philippians 4:13 quotations are from The Revised Standard Version of the Bible: Catholic Edition, copyright © 1965, 1966 the Division of Christian Education of the National Council of the Churches of Christ in the United States of America. Used by permission. All rights reserved.

Photographs appearing in *Sports and Faith: More Stories of the Devoted and the Devout* were supplied by Ave Maria University; Belmont Abbey College; *Chicago Tribune*; College of Holy Cross; De La Salle High School—Bob Sansoe of Sansoe Photography; Department of Defense—Raynel Emmons, U.S. Navy; Diocese of Springfield—Chuck Cherney Photo; Donovan Catholic High School; Eastern Michigan University; Library of Congress; Mississippi State University; Missouri State Archives; NASA; National Weather Service; St. Michael's Abbey—Rick Belcher, Photographer; Ron Meyer; Rob Sherwood; *Rockford Observer*; LancasterHistory.org; Notre Dame College Prep; Ypsilanti Historical Society; and Washington High School. Please see the Photographs and Illustrations Credit Table on page 225 for information.

The opinions and ideas expressed are those of the author who is entirely responsible for its content. The author has composed *Sports and Faith: More Stories of the Devoted and the Devout* at his own expense, using his own resources and technology. This publication is not associated in any way with the Chicago Bears Football Team.

Sports and Faith: More Stories of the Devoted and the Devout is Book 2 of the series.

Excerpt from "A Call" from OPENED GROUND: SELECTED POEMS 1966-1996 by Seamus Heaney. Copyright © 1998 by Seamus Heaney. Reprinted by permission of Farrar, Straus and Giroux, LLC.

— CONTENTS —

IF THE APOSTLES
HAD PLAYED FOOTBALL

If the Apostles had played football, they would have been a great team. Peter would have been the quarterback.

Andrew was Peter's brother. They would have been used to playing catch in the yard. Let's put Andrew at receiver.

James the son of Zebedee and his brother, John, were known as the sons of thunder. They would have been the running backs.

We don't know much about Philip, Bartholomew, James the son of Alphaeus, Thaddeus, and Simon the Canaanean. So they would have been the linemen.

Doubting Thomas would always be encouraging his teammates to play harder. Let's put him at middle linebacker.

Matthew the tax collector was used to dealing with money. Let's put him at end.

Matthias, who replaced Judas, would have been the kicker. The Apostles would have been excellent on special teams.

Paul would have been the writer. He wrote a lot of letters even though the Corinthians were the only ones who ever wrote back.

— Patrick McCaskey

BOB LADOUCEUR OF DE LA SALLE HIGH SCHOOL

— INTRODUCTION —

Welcome to *Sports and Faith Book 2: More Stories of the Devoted and the Devout* that follows four years after Book 1. My work with the Chicago Bears, Sports Faith International, and WSFI Radio helps keep me tuned in to sports and faith. The Chicago Bears are all about winning championships and serving the community. Sports Faith International honors high school, college, and professionals who lead exemplary lives. WSFI is all about faith and good works.

My grandfather, George Halas, was a positive person who continued with the Bears' franchise long after many other men would have given up. It did not take years for the Bears to become stable financially, it took decades. His legacy lives on—we persevere, we learn, we succeed.

There are plenty of stories of great athletes in *Sports and Faith Book 2* from current professionals like Jeremy Lin and Josh McCown, to legendary athletes like Stan "the Man" Musial and Bob Cousy. We also spotlight some great teams with lots of heart and courage. We look at Bob Ladouceur and his De La Salle teams that are portrayed in a new motion picture based on Neil Hayes's book, *When the Game Stands Tall*. And we spend some time with people like Tom Monaghan whose huge philanthropic concerns are known throughout the world and Guy Chamberlin, a great early NFL player and coach who quietly worked with troubled youths many years ago. We look at the University of Notre Dame, St. Michael's Norbertine Abbey, and other institutions that have a long religious history. We plunge into a few Bible stories. We take a look at some of the McCaskeys that you might find interesting. And I've included a few of my poems and creative writings.

We took on some sad developments. In this edition of *Sports and Faith* we look at the recent tragedy in Kabul where three brave men, Dr. Jerry Umanos and John and Gary Gabel were killed in cold blood. All three died at the foot of the cross. We look at the Washington, Illinois, tornado and the people who helped remediate the sufferings. And we also look at Burke Masters, Michael Lightner, and Grant Desme—three promising athletes who have followed in Father John Smyth's role of lifetime service.

ONE SPIRIT, ONE BODY

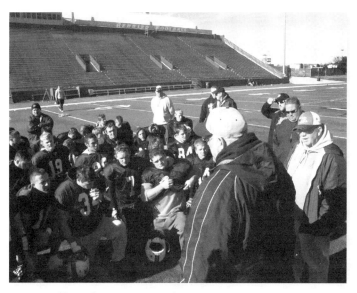

For in one Spirit were we all baptized into one body,
whether Jews or Gentiles, whether bond or free; and
in one Spirit we have all been made to drink.

— 1 Corinthians 12:13

DEADLY TORNADO IN WASHINGTON, ILLINOIS

On November 17, 2013, a deadly tornado struck Washington, Illinois, and the surrounding area. Two Washington residents died from the storm and 1,100 homes were damaged or destroyed. Nearly half of the houses in the town were affected. Immediately after the storm, many residents had to evacuate and come back several days later to determine if there was anything that could be salvaged.

TORNADO DAMAGE WASHINGTON, ILLINOIS

Neighbors helped neighbors. People consoled each other. They prayed. They made resolutions to rebuild. They ached for good to return—for signs of life—for signs of recovery and confidence. The Washington Community High School Panthers football team was scheduled to play the Sacred Heart-Griffin Cyclones the following weekend in Springfield. Washington Head Coach Darrell Crouch wanted his kids to overcome the adversity facing them. Washington would play the game—one way or another.

Before the playoff game, the Washington Community High School story was big news:

Washington Community High School plays in state play-off game after town is torn apart by a fierce tornado.

Coach Crouch would give his football players high marks at a pre-game press conference:

"Before we tried to organize our guys and get anything going (relief efforts), Coach Garcia, one of my assistant coaches was texting me. He was at church with three or four of our guys and as soon as they gave the all-clear they were out in the streets trying to help people out, getting people out of houses, helping the police go house-to-house. With athletics, we try to instill those things. We hope we build character, we hope we are building people who will be great leaders and when they come back to our community are going to be great fathers and husbands. Those guys' actions speak louder than words."

Outside Washington, Others Took Action

When the school reopens the following Thursday, parents and students from Joliet Catholic Academy bring pasta, salad, and other food to the Washington team football practice. Joliet Catholic parents and players also raise money for the relief efforts and many take part in helping Coal City and Diamond, other communities that had suffered from the storm as well.

Actions continued to speak louder than words from others who want to help.

The day after the storm, Sacred Heart-Griffin coach, Ken Leonard, whose team is scheduled to play Washington Community High School the following weekend at home in Springfield, calls Coach Darrell Crouch to find out what he needs. Within 24 hours, Leonard huddles up with his players, coaches, school administrators, and parents—they are all on board to help.

When Crouch tells Leonard that the team needs transportation, six buses are secured for players and fans. When Crouch tells Leonard that they need water, SHG friends and neighbors spring to action. Moms in minivans and other Springfield residents drop off water. Local businesses pitch in as well. A truck is dispensed to Washington with the goods. When Crouch tells Leonard that Washington needs money, the SHG locals donate generously. When Springfield parents hear about the Panthers' pregame tradition of dining on peanut butter and jelly sandwiches washed down with Gatorade, they buy the needed supplies. And then the moms collect food and drink to feed over 1,000 Washington fans for Washington's post game gathering. Businesses, friends, and strangers help in this gigantic effort.

The SHG swim team sets up for the post game event and the baseball team helps in the cleanup. SHG parents and a host of community volunteers help organize and serve the post-game meal. People give their time and talent generously. It all began with a phone call from Ken Leonard to Darrell Crouch.[1]

"BEARING UP"

In order to generate more awareness of the community needs after the tornado and to pitch in as concerned members of the greater community, 14 Chicago Bears' players and others from the organization came to Washington to help on December 4, 2013. The Bears visited the high school and did some cleanup. But mostly they helped lift the town's spirits and spent time with the high school kids. Financial contributions followed. Bears Care donated $210,194 to the Red Cross for their Illinois tornado relief fund. Bears fans helped generate $55,097 via donations and an online auction mostly of Bears' game-used and game-worn items. The Bears matched that total and provided an additional $100,000.

The Bears returned in June with a contingent of Bears' staff and supporters. This time the entire 2014 class of rookies led the effort. This trip included a flag-raising ceremony that featured patriotic songs and the Bears' fight song.

When there is work to be done after a catastrophe, teamwork can help take on big jobs. Athletes understand that there is strength in numbers and work together to accomplish great things.

BOB WETOSKA

Bob Wetoska was an excellent athlete and a remarkable team player. Wetoska was born in Minneapolis, Minnesota. He played football at DeLaSalle High School where he was all-state in his senior year. He was an Academic All-American at end for the University of Notre Dame which was named for God's mother. He played in the 1959 North South Game, the Senior Bowl, and the College All Star Game.

George Halas signed Bob Wetoska to the Bears when he was released by the Washington Redskins who had drafted him. Not flashy, but very reliable, Wetoska would perform yeoman's duty for the Bears, mostly at offensive tackle for the entire decade of the 1960s. At 6-foot-3 and 240 pounds, Wetoska was a natural guard, but he played tackle most of the time because that's where he was needed. He created holes for Gale Sayers and pass blocked for Bill Wade. He was good at it.

Wetoska was a key lineman for the Bears' 1963 Championship Team. He was team co-captain from 1965 through 1969. At the end of his career, the players coming up could help the team more than Wetoska so he told his coach it was time to move on and thanked him for having him on the team.

After Wetoska had retired from the Bears, *Chicago Sun-Times* sportswriter Jack Griffin wrote, "His face has that doughy quality often found in old time fighters, but there is a pleasant look about it. He is a quiet man, reserved, and with a gentleman's politeness."

Wetoska beautifully expressed his story of faith:

The Catholic Church teaches us that faith is a virtue, a gift from God that is instilled in each of us. An example proving this can be found in the gospel from last Friday's Mass which celebrated the Feast of the Chair of St. Peter. In the gospel, Jesus asks His disciples who the people were saying that Jesus was. They gave various answers like Elijah or one of the prophets, but Jesus said "Who do you say the Son of Man is?" Peter immediately responded "You are the Christ, the Son of God," and Jesus replied, "Blessed are you Simon for flesh and blood has not revealed this to you but my heavenly Father." While the gift of faith is instilled in each of us, it must be nurtured in order to survive, and thus we begin our journey of faith.

Everyone's journey of faith is different. For me it was quite straightforward. I was born into a practicing Catholic family, church every Sunday and holy day, meatless Fridays, fasting in lent etc. I was also given a Catholic education by Polish nuns and the Baltimore Catechism which began to form the foundations of my faith. It was in 3rd grade when the light bulb went on. I was making my First Communion on Mothers' Day in mid-May, trees were in bloom, flowers were coming up etc. When I got up that day, it was a bright sunny day but it had snowed during the night. My sisters were crying as we looked out the window but I thought it was beautiful, everything bright white and spotless, just like the slate that was wiped clean when I made my first confession the day before. Even at that young age, I knew that something very special, the Eucharist, was happening in my life that day. I felt that way then and still do, even to this day.

The next step in my journey of faith was attending DeLaSalle High School. The Christian Brothers were the biggest influence in the formation of my faith. Practical explanations of faith and morals, scripture study, the habit of daily prayer and living your faith all day every day. Each classroom session would begin with the words, "Let us remember that we are in the holy presence of God," a stirring thought. Prayer became an integral part of my daily life at DeLaSalle.

The final rung on my journey of the faith ladder was Notre Dame. Advanced religious studies, theology, Christian philosophy and ethics, daily Mass in the dorm, rosary at the Grotto, serving Mass in the Log Chapel and in the crypt beneath Sacred Heart Basilica for Father Hesburgh, a truly great faith foundation.[2] Catholic education nurtured my journey of faith, but with graduation it was time for me to take the ball and run with it. Needless to say, looking back on the past 75 years of my life, I've been tackled and gone down more often than I'd like to admit, but I've always been able to get up and continue the journey. God has answered my prayers and cries for help and has truly blessed every aspect of my life. I can find no other way to explain the success and tremendous gifts that I have received throughout my entire life.

I want to close with a true story of having faith in God and the power of prayer. Before Bear training camp began in 1962, my 4th year with the Bears, I decided to make a retreat. I was footloose and fancy free, having fun jobs between football seasons and enjoying the life of a single, young man. However, it dawned on me that I could sustain an injury in training camp and it would be bye bye Bears and welcome to the real world. I felt a retreat would begin the process of getting some real direction in my life. I prayed on a lot of things but there were two specific things I asked God to help me with. The first was that I would meet a woman of faith and values with the possibility of marriage in the future. Exactly one week later, completely by chance, a beautiful girl walked into my life and never left. She became my wife 48 years ago, the mother of our 5 wonderful children and grandmother of 16 grandchildren. She was truly a gift from God and I don't know where I would be without her.

The second thing I asked for at the retreat took a little longer, 15 months to be exact. I asked God to help me find a job that would prepare me for life after football. In October the following year, I gave a talk at the Our Lady of Perpetual Help Church Holy Name father and son meeting. After the meeting, a gentleman approached me and asked if I would consider interviewing for a job opening that he had available. I took the job, worked during our day off during the season and then during the off season so that when it came time for me to call it quits after the 1969 season,

*I had a permanent job. It turned out to be the only job
I ever had, buying the company from the principals
after 15 years and then selling it to my children before
I retired. My two retreat prayers were answered in
spades and my life has been a continuous stream of
blessings ever since. Jesus said, "Ask and you shall
receive." I asked. I received. I am a believer.*

Wetoska is Chairman of Wetoska Packaging Distributors in Illinois and Wetoska Packaging Sales and Service of Minnesota. In 2013, he was inducted into the Sports Faith International Hall of Fame. Wetoska has been on the board of advisors for the community and outreach services committee at Catholic Charities for over ten years. He has been an active supporter for Misericordia Heart of Mercy and other charities.

DAVE CASPER

Born in Bemidji, Minnesota, Casper played his first three years of high school football at St. Edward Central Catholic High School in Elgin, Illinois, and then finished high school at Chilton High School in Chilton, Wisconsin, where his team rolled over the competition. In eight games during the 1969 season, undefeated Chilton outscored its opponents 363–0. Casper attended the University of Notre Dame where he was the All-American captain of the 1973 team that was named national champion after it defeated the top-ranked Alabama team in the Sugar Bowl.[3] The great ND Coach Ara Parseghian called Casper the best athlete he ever coached.[4]

After graduating cum laude from Notre Dame with a degree in economics, Casper became one of the NFL's top tight ends. Selected in the second round by the Oakland Raiders in the 1974 NFL draft, Casper played with Oakland, Houston, Minnesota, and the Los Angeles Raiders. In *Football for Dummies*, fellow Raiders' Hall of Famer Howie Long lists Casper as one of the greatest offensive players of all time, writing:

> *"No tight end was more complete than Casper; he could block anyone and also find a crease, that tiniest of open spaces in the defensive secondary. He was very smart. When I think of wily veteran, I think of Dave Casper."*[5]

Ghost to Post and Holy Roller

When Casper played in Oakland with Ken Stabler as quarterback, he was one of three great receivers that gave opposing defenses fits. Joined by Fred Biletnikoff and Cliff Branch, Casper was next to impossible to contain if the defense was paying too much attention to the other receivers. Casper was nicknamed the "Ghost"[6] and in a 1977 playoff game against the Colts, running over the middle with his back to quarterback Ken Stabler, Casper caught a pass that sailed over his head and into his hands the way Willie Mays caught long drives in the outfield. The completion was called the "Ghost to the Post" play and is forever etched into NFL lore.

Casper was involved in another often discussed NFL play called the "Holy Roller." Early on in the 1978 season, the Raiders were down by 6 points to the Chargers with 10 seconds left in the game. The Raiders had the ball 15 yards outside the end zone. The ball was snapped to Stabler and he was immediately under pressure and about to be sacked. Stabler scooted the ball forward underhanded towards Pete Banaszak who was unable to recover it but scooted the ball forward where Casper made the recovery in the end zone. It was ruled a touchdown and the Raiders kicked the extra point for the 21–20 win. Rule changes followed and fumbles after the two-minute warning can only be advanced by the player who fumbled the ball.

Honors

The NFL allows fans, coaches, and players to elect the members of the Pro Bowl each year. Casper was elected five times in his career. The Press All Pro Team is selected by a national media members' panel. Casper was selected an All Pro four times. Over his 11 year NFL career, Casper had 378 receptions for 5,216 yards and 52 touchdowns. As a member of the Super Bowl XI Championship Oakland Raiders, he played with legendary greats Ken Stabler, Fred Biletnikoff, Cliff Branch, Art Shell, Gene Upshaw, and others. He was inducted into the Pro Football Hall of Fame and is also a member of the National Football Foundation College Football Hall of Fame, and the Sports Faith International Hall of Fame.

While the world admired Dave Casper for the intelligence, talent, and versatility that he brought to the game, he became equally loved for his virtues of humility, loyalty, and team play. Casper made it a practice to defer attention and praise to his team-mates. He considered himself a blocking tight end with modest receiving skills. Yet, he averaged more than 53 receptions for five consecutive seasons.

Beyond football, Dave Casper founded the Ronald Mc-Donald Celebrity Golf Tournament in Waconia, Minnesota. He is the recipient of the GTE All-American Academic Hall of Fame; NCAA Silver Anniversary award; and the Walter Camp Football Foundation Alumni of the Year. He is a member of Catholic Athletes for Christ and contributor to WSFI Radio. Casper and his wife Susan have three children. Casper is a Financial Adviser for Northwestern Mutual.

OLD TESTAMENT JOSEPH

What can we learn from Old Testament Joseph? His brothers hated him and he was unjustly put into prison. When he was successful, he gave the credit to God. When his family needed his help, he gave it to them abundantly and he didn't try to get revenge for their earlier mistreatment of him.

In a dream, Joseph and his brothers were binding sheaves in the field. Joseph's sheaf was in an upright position. The brothers' sheaves bowed to it. In another dream, the sun and moon and eleven stars bowed to Joseph.[7]

One day, Joseph's father, Jacob/Israel, sent Joseph to find his brothers who were tending flocks in Sheckem. When he got there a man told Joseph that his brothers had gone on to

Dothan. When Joseph arrived he found that his jealous brothers had plotted against him. Reuben cautioned his brothers not to kill Joseph. Instead, they threw him down a well. Judah suggested that Joseph be sold to some traders and he was.

Joseph's brothers took his tunic and put it into goat's blood. Jacob was led to believe that Joseph had been killed. Jacob was wracked with grief. Joseph was put in the very difficult position of having to report on his older brothers. It was natural for them to resent him. Still, they had no right to plot to kill him or throw him down a well or sell him to travelers.

What happened was heartbreaking. Only the grace of God could break the cycle of hatred and make the family whole again. Since the Lord was with Joseph, he was very successful when he became Potiphar's servant. Potiphar was the captain of the guards. Potiphar's wife tried to seduce Joseph, but she was unsuccessful. She lied to her husband who put Joseph in prison.

Joseph was in jail along with Potiphar's cupbearer and baker. He noticed they were disturbed about dreams that they could not interpret. Joseph was humble enough to know that dream interpretations come from God. Joseph was able to help others by letting God use him to interpret the dreams. Joseph's faith was tested. After the cupbearer was restored to favorable status with the pharaoh and was released from prison, he forgot Joseph.

Pharaoh dreamt about seven fat cows that were eaten by seven gaunt cows. He also dreamt about seven fat ears of corn that were swallowed by seven thin ears of corn. The dreams agitated Pharaoh. None of his magicians and sages could interpret the dreams. The chief cupbearer remembered his negligence of Joseph who correctly interpreted the dreams of the cupbearer and the baker. Joseph said that both Pharaoh's dreams had the same meaning. Seven years of abundance would be followed by seven years of famine. The dream was repeated because God reaffirmed the matter and God would make this happen soon.

Joseph suggested to Pharaoh that he put a wise person in charge of conserving the abundance for the famine years. Pharaoh put Joseph in charge of the operation. Pharaoh gave Joseph the name Zaphenath-paneah. He married Asenath. He was thirty years old when this took place. Their sons were Manasseh and Ephraim. Joseph traveled through Egypt. During the abundant years, food was stored. During the famine years, the stored food was distributed.

Hunger was felt throughout the land. People cried to Pharaoh who directed them to Joseph. God endowed Joseph with His spirit. God made his plan known to Joseph. God healed the wounds that Joseph suffered from his brothers. God made Joseph successful. After Jacob had heard that grain rations were available in Egypt, he sent ten of his sons there to buy grain. Benjamin stayed with Jacob. The ten brothers went to Egypt and bowed before Joseph because he was the prime minister. He recognized them, but they did not recognize him.

Joseph accused the ten brothers of being spies. He suggested as a test, one of the brothers could get Benjamin while the other nine were held in prison. Joseph amended his plan calling for just one of the brothers to be held in prison while the nine others brought grain home. Benjamin was to return to Joseph with the nine brothers. The nine brothers were surprised when they found the money paid for the grain had been returned to them in the grain bags. When the sons arrived home, Jacob did not want to send Benjamin back with the nine brothers.

Jacob's sons needed to return to Egypt because the famine became worse. They had also used the food that they had brought from Egypt. Joseph had told them to return with Benjamin, but Jacob did not want to do that. Reluctantly, Jacob told his sons to take gifts, extra money, and Benjamin to Joseph.

Joseph had an animal cooked for his brothers' dinner. They gave their gifts to Joseph. They bowed down before him. Joseph asked about Jacob. The brothers sat in order from the oldest to the youngest. Benjamin received five times more food than his brothers. Everyone had a wonderful time. The steward had received money from the brothers, but Joseph had told the steward to secretly give the money back to the brothers.

Joseph told his steward to give the brothers food for their people and their money back. Joseph also told the steward to put Joseph's goblet in Benjamin's bag.

After the brothers had left, Joseph told the steward to go after them and discover the goblet with Benjamin. The brothers came before Joseph who threatened to make Benjamin his slave. They all pleaded and at that point Joseph broke down, dismissed all his courtiers, and revealed himself to his brothers. Naturally, they all were shocked. Joseph tried to explain that it was God's way of saving the people, using their selling him into slavery to bring good in a time of need.

Pharaoh encouraged Joseph to bring his whole family to Egypt. He sent wagons to carry all the family members to their new land of plenty. Pharaoh and Joseph were very close. As they went back for their families and their father they had many gifts and food for Jacob. God reassured Jacob that he could go to Egypt with his whole family. Wives and children, livestock and possessions, sons and grandsons, daughters and granddaughters: all Jacob's descendants went to Egypt. Jacob's family amounted to seventy people.

Jacob sent Judah ahead of the caravan to meet Joseph. When he saw Jacob, Joseph flung his arms around Jacob's neck and wept openly with happiness. Since Jacob had seen Joseph alive again, he felt prepared for death.

KNUTE ROCKNE

SEASONS OF FAITH

For everything there is a season, and a time for every matter under heaven.

— *Ecclesiastes 3:1*

The McCaskey family is tied to several Christian churches over the generations—Presbyterian, Episcopalian, Lutheran, and Catholic. Many of my friends have similar backgrounds. The influence of an Irish Catholic grandmother on my dad's Scotch Irish side and a Bohemian Catholic coach on my mom's side helped bring the McCaskeys of my generation into the Catholic school system. Catholic schools in many areas made grade school football teams popular. Football continues with many Catholics into high school and college. I had to quit football after high school, but I would have loved to have played at the University of Notre Dame. Serious eye problems cut my play short. My time had come to seek something else. So over the decades I have been running in the Masters Track Circuit.

As my family and friends head into each new football season in the fall, we are reminded of the special affection we have for football. For those who played on or cheered for Catholic grammar school teams, who can forget the glorious Sunday games after church when the entire parish stood over at the park hugging the sidelines. The cheerleaders' sharp chant of "Push 'em back, push 'em back, waaaay back" still echoes today. On the field there was the knocking of helmets, blocking, tackling, and running like the wind amidst the cheers of what seemed like thousands.

The cheerleaders often got a better workout than the football players as homemade pompoms were thrust out in millions of quick moves, leaving thousands of tiny crepe paper streamers all over the field! And back when smoking was acceptable in public places, there was the strong smell of cigar smoke as dads and grandpas lit up just before the kickoff. Priests in their long cassocks and birettas would often find a good spot to watch the action and sometimes the Sisters would come over to the field as well.

In many places, Catholic grammar schools were the only grade schools to offer football—it was a truly Catholic school experience. Prayer was often a part of a team's "preparation" and if any player was injured, quiet prayer could be felt throughout the crowd. Grammar school football still goes on at many parishes and there are many Pee Wee teams. Most everyone has an opportunity to play or cheer.

UNIVERSITY OF NOTRE DAME

Catholics were once thought of as scruffy superstitious people by many other Americans and at many schools they were not welcome. Benjamin Franklin and others of the colonial period referred to Catholics as "Romans." Franklin would sometimes attend Mass and sit in the back of church as if he was studying a primitive culture and its practices.

A little college in South Bend, Indiana, grew into a great source of Catholic pride on the football field in the 1920s. The school was actually quite ecumenical with its players and coaches—you didn't have to be Catholic to play or coach the Irish. The great Knute Rockne did not become a Catholic until just before his son was to receive his First Communion when the coach had been at the school for several years. Rockne himself was impressed by his players whom he saw wake up very early on game day to attend Mass. On the road one day, Rockne could not sleep and went down to the hotel lobby where he saw player after player head out to church. He followed and he was impressed by his players' piety when he saw them receiving Communion. The players also seemed stronger and Rockne sought the same experience.[8]

Many of the fighting Irish are not Irish or Catholic, but it is wonderful to watch the singing of the "Alma Mater" after home games. Addressed to Our Lady, the patroness of the school, the song was composed by ND graduate Joseph Casasanta with lyrics written by ND President Father Charles O'Donnell. It was first performed at Knute Rockne's funeral in 1931. When singing the "Alma Mater," students of all nationalities and faiths put their arms over each other's shoulders and sway as they sing. Some smile and think nothing of the song's lyrics while others are obviously in prayer.

Some sports historians believe that it was Notre Dame under the great Knute Rockne that became the first "national team" in the college ranks. Rockne himself was so beloved and respected that when he died in a tragic plane crash in 1931, the entire nation mourned. Condolences came in to his widow from all over the world. Movies followed the Rockne legend and then more movies were made after more legends took shape. Notre Dame Football won national acclaim.

PROFESSIONAL RANKS

Some of the men who were involved in the early days of professional football were men of faith like my grandfather, George Halas. Tim Mara of the New York Giants and Art Rooney of the Pittsburgh Steelers passed on their faith to their heirs who run those teams today. Christian roots also run long and deep in the Green Bay Packers and the Arizona Cardinals as well. For decades, professional football was in such a delicate financial state, the early football pioneers needed great faith and courage just to hang on. In the Halas-McCaskey family, we believe there are great lessons to be learned from sports and we believe that faith directs everything you do in life, including sports.

Today, team members and coaches come from many different faiths. Each Sunday, a few hours before our games, Mass and chapel services are offered for the players. Players also organize Bible study groups that meet during the week. Charitable work is also an important part of many players' lives. The Bears and other teams encourage our athletes to give back to the community early and often. Our players share a common "faith" when they help clean up after tornadoes or build a Habitat for Humanity home.

On the Bears' plane, you might hear a lot of rough talk with athletes on the way to games, but you would also see my mother praying the Rosary during the flight.

As each new football season begins, there should be a certain satisfaction in what we have accomplished on and off the field in our great country. Like millions of other Americans, I get excited about football especially as a new season is about to start. And perhaps it is that optimism that makes the season begin with such joy.

ALWAYS LEARNING

I was always taking in the seasons and learning at Notre Dame Prep. I was in Coach Roach's American History class. I learned that the Gettysburg Address was a two-minute speech. The man who spoke before Lincoln talked for over two hours and no one remembers what he said.

When Coach Meyer had cordially invited me out for the track team, I accepted his invitation. (When I thanked him recently for letting me on the team, he said, "We let anyone on the track team.") The distance runners' coach, Father Devlin, said that I ran like a football player. I took that as a compliment.

In addition to running, I was interested in cycling. On a sunny, Sunday afternoon, I rode my bike 25 miles from

Des Plaines to Wheaton to see Louise Raymond…she wasn't home! The next day I had a half-mile race at Lake Forest High School. I didn't do very well.

For the conference meet at Saint Procopius, I was seeded 10th in the mile. The conference cross-country champion, Jack Duffy, was winning the mile. Then he fell and didn't continue the race. I counted the runners ahead of me. If I could finish fifth, I could get a medal and score a point. I did. We won the meet.

Father MacLoraine was the founding pastor of Saint Emily's Parish in Mount Prospect. My father came up with the idea of a fundraising record. On one side was famous big-band crooner Johnny Desmond singing "Ave Maria." On the flip side was a message from Father MacLoraine. Father MacLoraine had been an Army General and he was rather gruff. The gist of his message was "Hello. This is Father MacLoraine. We need money."

In the summer of 1966, I worked for Saint Emily's. I mowed the lawn and I painted classrooms. At the end of the summer, when Father MacLoraine paid me, he asked me, "What are you going to do with all of this money?"

I gave him an honest answer. I said, "I don't know."

Then he asked me, "Why don't you give it to Maryville?"[9]

I like to think that I quoted my mother and said, "We'll see."

My conscience bothered me for over 40 years. Then I wrote a check to the Ed McCaskey Scholarship Fund at Maryville Academy for $278.

LONG WAY HOME

At the 2014 Pro Bowl in Hawaii, my wife, Gretchen, and I had dinner with the Bears' Pro Bowlers Brandon Marshall, Matt Forte, Alshon Jeffery, Tim Jennings, Kyle Long, and their guests. Brandon Marshall led the grace before dinner. After dinner, I sang songs that I had written about each of the players.

It's a pleasure to get to know the Bears players. I am glad the Bears have Kyle Long. I wish we would have had his dad, Howie, when he played as well.

Howie Long was a very good football player, but he knew that he needed to be a better husband and father—football had taken all his attention during his Hall of Fame career. When he was 34 years old, he retired from the Raiders and settled down to focus most on family life while his kids were still young. Long's parents had divorced when he was young and for various reasons his home life fell apart. He lived with his grandmother, Elizabeth Mullan, and other family. Howie and most everyone in the family called Elizabeth, "Ma" and that's what she was to him. His uncles, the four Mullan brothers, made an impression on Long as well.

Long's early life in the Charlestown section of Boston was very difficult—his neighborhood was made up mostly of proud struggling Irish who worked very hard to make a living.[10] Developing a healthy self-esteem in Howie took a back seat to more immediate needs. Long's mother was ill and his father struggled to make a living. Young Howie was a big boy, but as a very young boy he was not predisposed to the kind of tough and tumble behavior that was common with many of his boyhood neighbors. A cousin encouraged, if not forced, a more bare-knuckle outlook and a fighting spirit developed.[11]

Long needed a change of environment and he was sent to live with his Aunt Aida and Uncle Billy in Milford, Massachusetts, where he attended high school. Unlike urban Charlestown, Milford was bucolic. Despite Long's tough beginnings, he was soft spoken and deliberate in speech; his grammar was excellent.

Long was a latecomer to organized football and only took it up in high school after he was encouraged to join the team by Dick Corbin, the Milford High School football coach. In Charlestown, Long had developed a truancy problem and those supporting him in Milford were doing their best to put an end to it. Long was an extraordinary athlete who played basketball and football in high school and also ran track. As school became more important to him, he applied himself. He attended Villanova University on scholarship, where he was a four-year letterman in football. He was also the Northern Collegiate boxing champion. After graduation, he married his college sweetheart, Diane Addonizio, who was tops in her class at Villanova. His wife would go on to law school and become an attorney.

HOWIE LONG ON HANGAR DECK OF THE USS HARRY S. TRUMAN

Long began his pro career as a second round draft pick of the Oakland Raiders in 1981 and he was highly motivated.[12] He contributed mightily to the 1983 Raiders' success and its 38–9 Super Bowl XVIII win over the Washington Redskins. The 6-foot-5, 268-pound defensive end had 5 tackles in the game and 13 sacks that season. In 1984, Long had 58 tackles and 12 sacks, and he was named the NFL Defensive Lineman of the Year. During Long's tenure with the Raiders, they would never reach the Super Bowl again, but they were always a force to be reckoned with. Among many football honors, Long was selected to eight Pro Bowls. He was inducted into the Pro Football Hall of Fame as a member of the class of 2000.

Since his playing career ended, Long has worked in television and the movies. Most recognizable for his role in Fox

NFL Sunday program with a cast of football greats. Long won an Emmy as Outstanding Sports Personality-Analyst Commentary in 1997. He has appeared in several movies including "Broken Arrow" with John Travolta. Commercials, sitcoms, voice roles in animated features, and sports hosting duties are part of Long's resume. He is also co-author of *Football for Dummies.*

Long looks back on his experience in football in a positive way. For Long, football provided a means for self-esteem, discipline, and respect. He believes that football can help provide structure in a young man's life, and experiences with a team are also very helpful. All three of Long's sons have played football.[13]

Long's sons, Chris and Kyle, have followed their dad into the NFL. Chris is a 6-foot-4, 275 pound defensive end for the Saint Louis Rams. Kyle is a 6-foot-6, 315 pound offensive lineman for the Chicago Bears. Both Long brothers are spirited players. A third son, Howard Jr., works for the Raiders in football operations.

Long was brought up as a Catholic and his grandmother was certainly a great influence on him. Despite being handsome, intelligent, and talented, Long grew up with many self-doubts. His accomplishments speak otherwise. His size comes from his 6-foot-8 father's side. Long was long on desire and work ethic and he also thanks others for his success:

"God gave me good people around me, and He gave me size. It's kind of a miracle, really."[14]

BOB COUSY WAKES UP BOSTON TO BASKETBALL

BOB COUSY

The Boston Celtics were not a very good basketball team before Bob Cousy arrived from Holy Cross in 1950. Cousy became the most beloved athlete in Boston. The "Houdini of the Hardwood" was a great ball-handler, passer, and shooter. He was only 6-foot-1, but he had speed and quickness, great peripheral vision, big hands, and long arms. He played for the Celtics from 1950-1963 and during that time he led the league in assists for eight years in a row and played in six championship seasons. His record breaking 28 assists in a single game that he set in 1959 held until 1978 when Kevin Porter got 29. He scored 16,960 points in his career—an average of 18.4 per game. He had 6,959 assists—an average of 7.5 per game. He averaged 5.2 rebounds per game and he held an .803 foul shooting percentage.

Cousy was an NBA All-Star every season he played and was named the All-Star Game Most Valuable Player in 1954 and 1957. He was named the NBA Most Valuable Player in 1957.

His play excited the Boston fans and the city developed a taste for the game. His 50 point performance in a playoff win against Syracuse in 1953 made an impression on fans that they simply never forgot. He went 30–32 at the free throw line and scored 12 points in the game's fourth overtime period.[15] Playing for the great coach Red Auerbach, Cousy was always passionate and driven to succeed. His behind-the-back dribbling and passing punctuated his approach that was part showman, part street ball, but all explosive. His passes were so quick and disguised that in the early days they bounced off his teammates' bodies and heads. When Cousy had the ball, everyone on the court was challenged to "stay in" the game every second. When Bill Russell came to Boston in the 1956 draft, the Celtics' championships seasons began. They won 6 out of 7 championships with Cousy and Russell. Then Russell and the Celtics won 5 out of 6 championships after Cousy's retirement.

In the "Vision Books" series for children, Bob Cousy is portrayed in a book called *Champions in Sports and Spirit* by Ed Fitzgerald. Cousy came from a French immigrant family of limited means and he never forgot those who struggled around him. His faith was fundamental. In *Champions in Sports and Spirit*, Cousy is quoted:

"While I was at Holy Cross, I received Holy Communion on an average of three times a week for the whole four years, and I feel that any success I may have had at school and since my graduation can be attributed to the religious foundation I was able to build there."

Cousy's family home is in Worcester, Massachusetts, where he and his wife Marie raised their two daughters, Marie Colette and Mary Patricia. Bob and Marie brought their daughters up with a strong sense of social justice that included attending civil rights rallies. Cousy called his wife "Missy," and while he was frequently away due to his demanding playing and coaching career, he was absolutely devoted to her. Missy began suffering from dementia about the year 2000 after 50 years of marriage. Cousy put his husband skills in overdrive and did everything he could to care for his wife and see that her remaining years were comfortable—helping her maintain a healthy routine, fixing her medication, reading the newspaper with her, and taking care of her needs for over 12 years of decline. She passed away in 2013.

Boston fans who were around during Cousy's playing career will remember Cousy's Celtics farewell ceremony on Saint Patrick's Day of 1963. It was his final regular-season game at home in Boston on the way to another championship. As Cousy was choking back tears during his goodbye speech, a fan shouted out, "We love ya, Cooz." Tears flowed and applause followed for one of Boston's most beloved athletes.

Cousy received an honorary doctorate of humane letters from Boston College in 2014. In honor of the great guard, the Bob Cousy Award is given to the top collegiate male basketball point guard annually by the Naismith Memorial Basketball Hall of Fame.

JAMIE MOYER'S MANY SEASONS

Jamie Moyer is a veteran of 27 seasons in professional baseball. His career was not only long, but unconventional in many ways. Originally selected by the Chicago Cubs in the sixth round of the 1984 draft, Moyer was well-known for his ability to change speeds at will and locate every pitch. He challenged modern hitters by pitching in ways that made them uncomfortable at the plate. There is nothing quite so frustrating for muscular aggressive hitters to miss pitches that are slow and inside. Moyer was known to throw an 80 mph fastball and a 60 mph changeup!

Moyer's talent was not extraordinary for a major league pitcher; he struggled at times to just stay in the lineup, but he improved with age. He was actually a better pitcher in his 40s than his 20s.

Pitching careers can run short. Moyer was cut by the Texas Rangers holding a career 34–39 record at the start of the 1991 season. He moved on to St. Louis where he was 0–5 for the Cardinals. He was 29 when he dropped down to the Toledo Mud Hens in 1992.[16] For most athletes this would have been time to get another job, but not Moyer.

When things got rough for Moyer, he got going. He received invaluable consul from baseball guru Harvey Dorfman. Although not a psychiatrist, Dorfman became baseball's top consultant to players who needed to regain their edge. In Dorfman's practice, he showed tough love and kept the responsibility squarely on the player's back to fix problems. Dorfman helped, but Moyer had to do his own fixing.

Moyer worked his way back to the big leagues and pitched three years for Baltimore from 1993-1995. He split time between Boston and Seattle in 1996 when he was 13–3.

He stayed in Seattle where he found stability for the next ten seasons pitching well. During the 2006 season, he moved on to Philadelphia and had a good run for the Phillies into the 2010 season when he severely injured his arm. Once again, he faced the end of his career, but he did not quit. He had Tommy John Surgery[17] to repair his arm and played for Colorado in 2012; he went 2–5. Still, Moyer did not want to retire, but a new TV sportscaster contract to cover Phillies games finally put an exclamation point on the end of a prolific pitching career. Moyer's final pitching record is 269–209.

Over the course of his career, Moyer earned numerous honors for his character, commitment to others, and professionalism. His honors include the Roberto Clemente Award, the Lou Gehrig Award, the Branch Rickey Award, Sporting News Number 1 MLB Good Guy, Dallas Green Special Achievement Award, the Steve Patterson Award, and many others.

Moyer and his wife Karen have eight children and are devout Catholics and philanthropists. They established and run the Moyer Foundation, a non-profit organization dedicated to helping children in severe distress. With the community's support, the Moyer Foundation has raised more than $19 million to support over 200 hundred different programs that directly serve the needs of children in distress. HBO produced a compelling documentary called "One Last Hug" on the Moyer Foundation's Grief Camp for Kids, which aired in April, 2014.[18]

WEDDING SONGS AND PRO BOWL REPORTS

Like Bob Cousy and Jamie Moyer I try to be a good husband.

A SPOUSE'S LAMENT
[Either the husband or the wife can sing this.]
I never get to do
What I want to do
It's always "Honey do this."
I never get to do
What I want to do
It's always "Honey do that."
I have to do everything
I have to do everything
It's really unfair
But what do I care
I have to do everything

Then we pray together
And we remember
God does most of the work

— Patrick McCaskey

In 1941, Al Hoffman wrote the song "Bear Down, Chicago Bears." In 1959, Andy Williams recorded "Hawaiian Wedding Song." Al Hoffman was one of the writers. In 1979, the Pro Bowl was in Los Angeles. My grandfather, George Halas, my uncle, Mugs Halas, and my father, Ed McCaskey, didn't want to go. So they sent me. I got to meet Pro Football Hall of Famer Lamar Hunt.[19]

In 1984, Gretchen did me a big favor; she married me. We went to Hawaii for our honeymoon and the league meeting. In 2014, we went to the Pro Bowl in Hawaii. As an anniversary gift to each other, we traveled business class. At the Pro Bowl Mass, the priest asked for volunteers to be lectors. I was the only one.

The game was competitive and good. Our seats were beneath an overhang. So we didn't get wet during the rain. After the game, the bus driver went the wrong way. We got to travel on a highway that was an amazing example of engineering. I thought of my grandfather, George Halas, who was an engineering major. Gretchen and I stayed at the Disney Hotel because Walt Disney was from Chicago. At our last supper in the Disney Hotel, strolling musicians serenaded us with "Hawaiian Wedding Song."

In the January/February 2014 issue of "The Atlantic," William Deresiewicz published an article entitled "The Jewish

Mark Twain." It was about Sholem Aleichem and two books about him: "The Worlds of Sholem Aleichem: The Remarkable Life and Afterlife of the Man Who Created Tevye" by Jeremy Dauber and "Wonder of Wonders: A Cultural History of Fiddler on the Roof" by Alisa Solomon. I finished reading both books on the trip. Mark Twain said that he was the American Sholem Aleichem. Deresiewicz wrote that Tevye was Job with a punch line.

On the night flight home, I got to see the movie "Young Frankenstein."[20] After we had landed at Chicago O'Hare, I gave Gretchen a ride home. Then I went to Halas Palace and filed this report.

TUESDAY, NOVEMBER 10, 1998

During the night, there was a heavy rainstorm.

So we woke up tired.

In the morning, right after my wife, Gretchen, left for Community Bible Study, a lady from Saint Mary's School called to say that there was a

Power failure.

There was no school.

My sons, Edward – 12, Thomas – 9, and James – 7, said that it was okay

For me to go to work.

So I was immediately suspicious.

After I had gone to work, they went in the backyard and leaned

Backwards into the wind.

They did not fall down.

I came home for lunch and found popcorn and soda remnants.

After Gretchen had returned from CBS, the power in our house went out.

So the boys played front yard football in the wind.

Then a deliveryman brought a carton that was clearly marked "Foosball."

It was a Christmas present for James.

It did not need electricity.

So we celebrated Christmas early.

I went back to work.

It was too windy to pick up all the willow branches that were on the ground.

We went out to dinner because the power was still out.

As we approached our neighborhood on the drive back, Edward said, "If the power is on, I'll praise the Lord.

If it's not, I'll be very angry."

I replied, "You've got the first part right."

As we got out of the car in the driveway, the power went back on.

The boys played computer football.

The Bears won.

At bedtime, Edward played Michael W. Smith's Christmas compact disc. Thomas said, "It's going to be a long night. He's got that 'Christmastime' song on 'repeat.'"

After Edward had learned the song, he turned it off.

— Patrick McCaskey

Prayer and Work

CHALLENGER CREW

Not to desire to be called holy before one is; but to be holy first, that one may be truly so called.

To fulfil daily the commandments of God by works.

To love chastity. To hate no one. Not to be jealous; not to entertain envy. Not to love strife.

Not to love pride. To honor the aged. To love the younger. To pray for one's enemies in the love of Christ.

To make peace with an adversary before the setting of the sun. And never to despair of God's mercy.

— Rule of St. Benedict

The Rule of Saint Benedict has been a fundamental guide for monastic life for many centuries. Saint Benedict lived around 500 AD and *Saint Benedict's Rule* has since served as a guide for those who wanted to live in community and in faith. The term "ora et labora" (prayer and work) describes the Benedictine way in a nutshell. *Saint Benedict's Rule* encourages community members to avoid idleness and directs them to spend their time in prayer, labor, and sacred reading. The "Rule" advocates a balance in life that keeps people on task.

Of course, many Christians keep busy outside of monasteries. We are not all meant to be monks, ministers, or other Religious, but we can forge a kind of life of prayer and labor. Many of the best in sports have done just that.

BEARS AND THE SPACE SHUTTLE

The 1985 Bears were one of the greatest teams in NFL history. But, it wasn't until October 7, 2011, President Obama welcomed the 1985 Super Bowl Champion Chicago Bears to the White House to celebrate their Super Bowl victory. In 1986, the team's White House reception was canceled because of the Space Shuttle Challenger tragedy.

Super Bowl XX was played on January 26, 1986 at the Louisiana Superdome in New Orleans. The Chicago Bears clobbered the New England Patriots, 46–10. Bears defensive end Richard Dent was named the game's most valuable player.

Two days after the Bears Super Bowl win, the Space Shuttle Challenger broke apart 73 seconds into its flight, leading to the deaths of all seven crew members. The disaster was blamed on an O-ring seal that failed at liftoff. Christa McAuliffe, the first member of the Teacher in Space Project and the first regular U.S. civilian space traveler was killed in the disaster. Many school children across the country were watching Challenger's liftoff.

President Reagan was scheduled to deliver a "State of the Union" speech on that night. Instead, he delivered a tribute to the lost astronauts.

One particularly poignant thought by the President:

> *''For those who knew you well and loved you, the pain will be deep and enduring. A nation, too, will long feel the loss of her seven sons and daughters, her seven good friends. We can find only consolation in faith, for we know in our hearts that you who flew so high and so proud now make your home beyond the stars, safe in God's promise of eternal life.''*

BISHOP CANEVIN BASEBALL TEAM EXCELS

Bishop Canevin High School in Pittsburgh is a Catholic co-educational, college-preparatory institution. The school has great ambitions for its students—in what they will achieve as well as what they will become. Everyone at the school works hard toward their goals.

Students at Bishop Canevin strive for excellence in academics, service, and athletics. Athletes excel both on and off the field. Each year the baseball team completes a service project to help out the local communities. As part of its "Going Beyond the Diamond" program, the team raised $2,100 in a fundraiser for the Pittsburgh Fallen Heroes fund. The team also collects toys and other items to help the Ronald McDonald House. Student athletes visit the Ronald McDonald House to have lunch with the families and spend time with the kids.

Bishop Canevin High School prepares students for a life anchored in faith, a life enlightened by learning, and a life committed to the promotion of charity and justice. Rooted in the Gospel of Jesus Christ and aligned with the principles of Ignatian spirituality, the school challenges students to life-long learning and growth in a spirit of "competence, conscience and compassion."

Founded upon the call of Jesus Christ to be people of love and life, students come to possess individual integrity, social responsibility, and a Christian response to the secular culture of our time. Students are taught that all persons, created in the image and likeness of God, are worthy of dignity, respect, and reverence. They regard all creation as sacred, deserving their respect, protection, and care.

The Bishop Canevin High School Baseball team was named Sports Faith International's High School Team of the Year in 2011. Prior to the award, the Crusaders qualified for the playoffs in 20 out of 21 seasons. Coach Dale Checketts said he was especially proud to win the Sports Faith International award because it recognizes all that the team does off the field.

STAN "THE MAN" MUSIAL

STAN MUSIAL

Some players in sports will be remembered in a special way, such as how they lived their lives and looked out for others. Stan Musial was one of these.

Beloved in St. Louis, Musial was a tremendous force for good in baseball and in life. And to the everlasting consternation of his fans, he is often overlooked in discussions of the greatest baseball players today. St. Louis sports writers suggest that Musial's image and reputation have grown dim outside the Gateway City. Yet, he certainly has the affection of St. Louisans. They don't call him Stan "the Man" Musial for nothing. In St. Louis, he is celebrated.

According to Baseball Commissioner Bud Selig who knew and appreciated Stan Musial:

> *Baseball is a social institution and we've been blessed that our great players, for the most part, have been great human beings. There can't be anybody better than Stan Musial. Just can't. Not possible.[21]*

Musial was born on November 21, 1920 in Donora, Pennsylvania. He was the son of Lukasz Musial, a Polish immigrant and Mary Lancos Musial, a girl of Czech descent.[22] While not much of a student, Musial was destined to be a professional athlete. Working in the mills was the regular vocation of men in the area; Musial looked to sports.

Chuck Schmidt, a local baseball player who helped Musial's high school coach, called Musial "a born natural" whom "God" made great.[23] Along with sports, Musial found love at an early age. On his nineteenth birthday, November 21, 1939, Musial eloped with Lillian Labash. They had a long happy marriage.

Musial began his baseball career as a pitcher, but after he had injured his shoulder, he moved to the outfield and first base. When he began his pro career as a teenager in the Minors, he dealt with very difficult financial times. He was one of thou-

sands of good athletes trying to make it in professional baseball. Encouragement came from his wife and Dickie Kerr, his
manager at Daytona Beach. His father-in-law pitched in to help
support Musial's young family as the minor leaguer worked his
way into the big leagues.

Once Musial played for the big-league Cardinals in 1941,
his financial circumstances changed quickly and within a few
years, he was making an excellent salary that continued to rise
for many years. After spending 1945 in the Navy working in
a ship repair unit, he was back in the Majors in 1946.

His Cardinal career is one of year-after-year excellence,
awards, and records. Over his long career, he was incredibly consistent. In 1943, he held the highest batting average
in the National League at .357. He held it as well in 1946,
1948, 1950, 1951, 1952, and again in 1957. He was an All
Star 24 times.[24]

Musial played for 22 seasons and he holds an incredible career batting average of .331. He hit home runs, 475
of them. He hit 725 doubles and 177 triples. He finished
his career with 1,951 RBIs and 1,949 runs. He was fast in
the field and on the base path. He was also a tremendous
clutch hitter. Opposing teams feared Musial and his cork-
screw stance that peppered winning line drives throughout
his long career. Musial was inducted into the National
Baseball Hall of Fame in 1969.

Vin Scully, the venerable sportscaster, was asked to describe just how good Musial was and he put it this way:

Good Enough to Take Your Breath Away

Coaches, fans, and opposing teams could also count on his performance day in and day out. George Will pointed out that Stan Musial had "amazing consistency—he got 1,815 hits on the road and 1,815 at home—and it made him unspectacularly spectacular."

Stan Musial was also consistently Christian in his behavior. He regularly attended Mass and treated those around him with respect. He attended other players' funerals, even when it required extensive travel and sacrifice when he was older.

Musial is one of the top ten hitters in baseball history. And he was exceptional when taking time out to sign autographs, chat, and acknowledge his fans. Famous for having a pocketful of signed cards for giving unprepared fans that he met, Musial also loaded up his car's trunk with memorabilia that he would generously give away. Some Saint Louis fans joke that everyone in the city owns a card signed by Musial.

Stan "the Man" had a good sense of humor and was also a joy to be around. Baseball catchers are famous for chatting up batters so they lose their concentration at the plate. One of the best at such chatter was Joe Garagiola. When Garagiola was catching for the Pirates and Musial stepped up to the plate, he attempted to distract him.

Musial owned a restaurant and Garagiola tried to rattle him in this way. Before the first pitch, Garagiola told Musial to expect 10 of Garagiola's buddies at his restaurant that night. Strike One! Before the second pitch, Garagiola asked

Musial about the best way to get to the restaurant. Strike Two! When the third pitch came along, Musial shut out the noise and knocked the ball over the wall for a home run. Coming to home plate, Musial paused long enough to ask Garagiola, "How do your people like your steaks?"[25]

Musial was famous for playing his harmonica, which became a trademark for him. He played it when he was out in public to amuse fans and he played it at hospitals when visiting the sick. He played his rendition of "Take Me Out to the Ball Game" at the National Baseball Hall of Fame. He also played his harmonica on the TV show, "Hee Haw."

Musial appeared on a number of TV shows such as the sitcom "That Girl" with Marlo Thomas, and "What's My Line" where panelists, sometimes blindfolded, guess at the identity of the guests. He appeared with Merv Griffin and Ed Sullivan. Musial graced the cover of eight *Sports Illustrated* issues and he was often a guest on sports shows and televised sporting events. President Lyndon Johnson named Musial National Director of the President's Council on Physical Fitness.

Musial was an ambassador for baseball, demonstrating the best qualities of its players. Upon Musial's retirement, Commissioner Ford Frick captured something of the man in his remarks:

> *Here stands baseball's perfect warrior. Here stands baseball's perfect knight.*

Musial received the Cavalier Cross of the Order of Merit from the Polish government and the Presidential Medal of

Freedom from President Obama. A quiet man of faith, Musial remarked once that although he didn't see anything wrong with athletes making the Sign of the Cross during competition:

> *I found a better way a long time ago. Every day that I possibly can I go to Mass and Communion. There I make my Morning Offering and that way you can even turn an error into a prayer.*[26]

He was a friend to many Religious including Pope Saint John Paul II. Many more were impressed by his ways. Among those charities that he supported: Covenant House Missouri, which provides services to at-risk youth; Villa Duchesne and Oak Hills School; and Christian Brothers College High School.[27] Musial was posthumously inducted into the Sports Faith International Hall of Fame in 2014.

When it was announced that Bishop Timothy Dolan was selected by the Pope to become Cardinal, he was asked if he had ever "wanted to be a cardinal."

> *Yes, when I was six years old. I wanted to be Stan Musial!*

Cardinal Dolan lauded Stan Musial this way:

> *Alleluia! A great man! A superb athlete! Married seven decades to his beloved Lil; proud father; committed Catholic (he readily admits one of the highpoints of his life was getting to know his fellow Pole, Blessed John Paul II); never missed Sunday Mass; no steroids*

*or drugs; no brawls, enemies, or DUI. Just a gentle-
man, day-in-day-out reliable, never complaining or demanding; no controversy or foul language. And one of
the best baseball players ever, an inspiration to generations, whose very name stands for integrity, professionalism, loyalty, and championship...We need more Stan
Musials. He makes me proud to be a "cardinal."[28]*

My Work in Progress

PATRICK McCASKEY AT NOTRE DAME COLLEGE PREP
COMMENCEMENT, MAY 31, 2014

Tom Bunzol, Dick Rafferty, and I were an intramural three-man basketball team at Notre Dame of Niles Prep. We won every game. We had to play during the second half of our lunch hour because the school basketball teams needed the gym to practice after school. We only had one gym.

There was barely time to eat lunch, hop into a pair of sneakers, play the game, jump back into my street clothes, and make it to my first afternoon class. One particular afternoon, after a hard-fought victory, I was very sweaty and tired. My shirt was hanging out, not only because I was sloppy, but also to cover the pockets of my Levi's that were illegal to wear. I barely made it to study hall before the second bell rang.

Since I was so physically exhausted, I merely laid my books on my desk and laid my head on top of them in the fond hope of falling immediately asleep. However, the study hall monitor was a strict disciplinarian and he had other plans for me. He roused me from my deep sleep and commanded me to free my mind to God's will by disciplining it through study.

Then I discovered how dry my mouth was. Barely audible, I said, "I thirst."

The study hall monitor realized that I was sinful and separated from God. Since he cared about me, he wanted me to know God's love and God's wonderful plan for my life.

So he wrestled me out of my desk. My response was, "My God, my God, why hast thou forsaken me?"

In an attempt to prove to me that "the wages of sin is death," the study hall monitor took me by my shirt collar and brought me into the hallway. Father Schuneman happened to be walking by. The study hall monitor said to him, "Maybe you can do something with McCaskey."

Father Schuneman didn't say anything for a long time. He waited for me to say something. In the interim, The Holy Spirit worked a miracle in my life. I felt compassion and understanding for the study hall monitor. His behavior was not a problem; it was an opportunity to show God's love. I came down to his level to help him, just as Christ became man to save us, so many football seasons ago.

I said to Father Schuneman, "Father, forgive him for he knows not what he does."

The entire incident earned me a Saturday detention. "It is finished."

WORKING AT ALPHA EPSILON PHI

For my last two semesters at Indiana University, I lived in Alpha Epsilon Phi Sorority with seventy ladies as their house-boy. I heard that the job was open and I took that as a mandate.

These were very intelligent young women, but I felt the need to encourage their cultural development. I had covers of "The New Yorker Magazine" on my bedroom walls. If a lady could find the two covers that were identical, she could stay longer. The identical covers were next to each other.

I had never lived in a sorority before. When I first went there, I thought that living there would be my life's answer to "Walden." I told the housemother that I was happy when I was working. She kept me very happy.

I had the opportunity to mow the grass, shovel the snow, push cars out of the parking lot, take the dirty linen downstairs, take the clean linen upstairs, haul the garbage, replace burned out light bulbs, fix towel racks, repair furniture, fix closet doors, take empty pop bottles downstairs, fill the pop machine, stock the pantries, and sweep and mop the large dining and kitchen floors nightly. I did not shrink from these challenges; I welcomed them. I received room, board, and $22 a month. My room was known as "Luxury Manor."

During my first sorority semester, in the fall of 1973, my writing professor, Scott Sanders, suggested that I start my own humor publication. So I mimeographed my writings for the ladies.[29] Each Thursday night, after midnight, I put an essay or a poem in their mailboxes.

During my second sorority semester, in the winter and spring of 1974, after I had found out that I was allergic to duplicating fluid, I performed collections of my writings on Friday evenings in the dining hall while the ladies were eating desserts. My oral interpretation professor, Doctor Hawes, had each student choose a writer for their concert reading at the end of the semester. I chose me. I still have evaluation notes from my classmates and my teacher. I gave up living in a sorority to work for the Chicago Bears.

DIFFERENT TESTS

As a 5-10 eighth grader,
I had to choose
between basketball and speedskating.
Basketball had cheerleaders.
After high school and only three more inches,
I had to give up football
because of eye problems.
So I ran cross-country.
After two seasons,
I had to give up cross-country
because of allergy problems.
So I wrote humor.
After ten years,
I became immune to many allergies,
but not kryptonite.
So I started running again.
My test was easier than Job's.
His was essay.
Mine was multiple choice.

— Patrick McCaskey

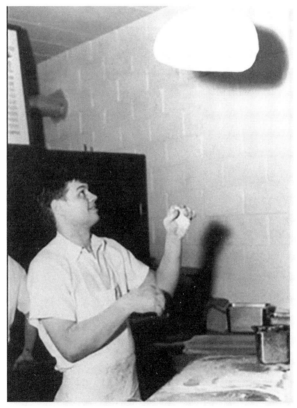

TOM MONAGHAN, TOSSING PIZZA DOUGH

PERSEVERANCE

AVE MARIA UNIVERSITY

Grant me, O Lord my God, a mind to know you, a heart to seek you, wisdom to find you, conduct pleasing to you, faithful perseverance in waiting for you, and a hope of finally embracing you.

— Saint Thomas Aquinas

L ife is difficult and it takes strong effort to continue on track towards our goals and aspirations. Regardless of how difficult it may get or how we may suffer along the way, we must remain steadfast in our journey. There are many examples of how athletes and others keep on track or fall off in both their competitive engagements and their pursuit of something of a higher calling.

Josh McCown Perseverance

The Chicago Bears handed out their 2014 Piccolo Awards in the morning on Tuesday May 6, 2014 at Halas Hall in Lake Forest, Illinois. Both a Bears' rookie and a veteran are selected by teammates for the award each year. The recipients display the courage, loyalty, teamwork, dedication, and sense of humor exemplified by Brian Piccolo.

The Bears right tackle Jordan Mills was awarded the Brian Piccolo Award for a Bears rookie. Mills helped solidify the Bears offensive line that had been considered the most serious weakness prior to the 2013 season. Mills is considered by teammates as one of the most dedicated and hard-working players who displays humility and a willingness to learn. The consummate dedicated athlete and team player, Mills thanked the Bears for the honor.

Former Bears-now-Cleveland quarterback Josh McCown received the Piccolo award given to a veteran Bears' player. McCown, who has served many teams in the NFL, helped solidify the Bears offense when Jay Cutler was out for a large part of the 2013 season. Cutler spoke at the ceremony, pointing out that McCown took on his backup job with a determination and commitment that was exemplary. McCown did many extra unselfish things to help the team and those around him play better. McCown is the kind of player who thinks of others in every circumstance.

McCown's story is also interesting in that he has toiled for many years in the midst of anonymity and job insecurity that comes with a backup role in the NFL. There is something of Old Testament patience in Josh McCown. He was drafted by the Arizona Cardinals in 2002. He played backup to Jake Plummer his first year. He played backup to Jeff Blake his second year. He started his third year and although his completion percentage and quarterback rating was an improvement over the previous starters, it was not good enough.

Perhaps there is no other position in the NFL as tenuous as backup quarterback. Teams have a difficult time keeping three quarterbacks on a team. In today's fast paced game, the team may see injuries to their starter. In 2005, the Cardinals signed on magnificent-though-aging Kurt Warner. One can hardly imagine the excitement on the Cardinals team when they were able to team Warner with superstar receiver Larry Fitzgerald. The Cardinals offense moved up towards the middle of the pack quickly, but the defense sunk like a stone to give the team a 5–11 record. When McCown headed east to Detroit in 2006, he was backing up Jon Kitna who was becoming well traveled himself in the league. After starting nine games in Oakland in 2007, McCown went to Carolina in 2008-2009 as a backup there. McCown was out of the NFL in 2010 and came back to the Bears in 2011, where he was third in the rotation. He was cut in 2012 and then re-signed in November.

Something remarkable happened in 2013. McCown did more than backup Jay Cutler in 2013. He replaced Cutler for half the season and the Bears' offense did not skip a beat. Both quarterbacks led the Bears to an excellent offensive year, but defensive weaknesses dragged the team down. McCown completed 149 passes on 224 attempts for a 66.6 completion percentage with 13 touchdowns and only one interception. He finished with an amazing 109 quarterback rating. His stingy single interception would have made him a hero on many Bears' teams of lore. In the 1960s, when the Monsters of the Midway defense turned over the field to the offense, they were sometimes known to admonish their offensive teammates to not give up a touchdown. The defense was so confident in their abilities; they thought they could score enough themselves to win.

McCown moved on to play for the Tampa Bay Buccaneers under Lovie Smith in 2014. He signed a three-year deal with the Cleveland Browns in 2015. Whatever happens for the remaining of McCown's career, the team that carries him on the roster will have a player who is willing to work with those around him and do the best for his team.

When away from the NFL in 2011 and 2012, McCown worked as an assistant coach at Marvin Ridge High School in Waxhaw, North Carolina. And although McCown leapt back onto professional football, his ambitions go beyond being a great quarterback.

McCown spent a season alongside one of the most popular Christian athletes, Kurt Warner. For McCown, Warner was a guy "who walked the walk." While McCown has admired other Christian athletes, he knows there are great temptations. McCown has talked about how some players give praise one game and then are arrested a week later. True faith helps fight off temptation and more. McCown draws on faith for his source of strength in perseverance in the NFL and the other parts of his life.

McCown is a positive influence in the locker room and outside football. He is on the board of directors for Pro Athletes Outreach an organization that recognizes and addresses the challenges of integrating faith, family, and career that pro athletes face today. He led the Bears' Bible study and worked with the author in the Bears' community development activities. He is a man who inspires his teammates and many others, but it has not been easy. For McCown, it required faith and perseverance—the kind you read about in the Old Testament.

A TIMELINE

In 1852, Harriet Beecher Stowe published "Uncle Tom's Cabin."

In 1862, Abraham Lincoln met her and asked "Is the little woman who made this great war?"

In 1865, Lincoln said, "Both (sides) read the same Bible, and pray to the same God; and each invokes His aid against the other."

In 1974, I started working for the Bears, and the players went on strike.

In 1982, I received a promotion, and the players went on strike.

In 1987, I bought a house, and the players went on strike.

In 2011, I published "Sports and Faith," and the players signed a new collective bargaining agreement.

Tom Monaghan Cooks up a Crusade

Tom Monaghan had many struggles in early life. He was born March 25, 1937 in Ann Arbor, Michigan. His younger brother, Jim Monaghan, followed two years later.[30] His father died on Christmas Eve when Monaghan was just 4 years old. His mother suffered from what would be called bipolar disorder today and struggled to raise her energetic boys. She put the boys into foster care and then sent them to Saint Joseph's Home for Boys, an orphanage in Jackson, Michigan. Monaghan found life at Saint Joseph's oppressive although beneficial. He developed a strong Catholic faith at the orphanage in his six year stay. He remembered with particular fondness, Sister Berarda, a Felician nun, who was especially encouraging and supportive.

In addition to his growing faith, Monaghan also developed a love for architecture at stately old Saint Joseph's, which had originally been a mansion. He hoped to study architecture at the University of Michigan, but he was never able to advance his education beyond two years of study.

His mother brought the boys back to live with her in Traverse City, Michigan, where she had moved. Again, she found it difficult to manage the young Tom Monaghan and he was sent to foster care. He lived and worked on farms and enjoyed the hard work and discipline of farm life. Occasionally, he would settle in with relatives for periods of time. But, there was no security in Monaghan's very young life and even less in his adolescent life.

After graduating from high school and moving around for jobs, Monaghan found himself in Harvey, Illinois, without a penny. On a whim, or perhaps out of desperation, he entered a recruitment office and joined the Marines thinking that he was in fact enlisting in the Army. He would later say that the extra discipline and struggle that he experienced in the Marine Corps was an unplanned benefit. He came out a better man, but naïve in the ways of the world. He was separated from his Marine Corps savings in a swindle. He returned to Ann Arbor and eventually bought into the pizza business in Ypsilanti with his brother, Jim. He seemed perfectly suited for the pizza business. He was especially polite and appreciative of his customers—after all, they were feeding him and he had times in his life when food was scarce. He was also athletic, energetic, competitive, and intellectually curious about things that could play a positive role in his life. All these things contributed to his success. His brother on the other hand, was not the risk-taker that Tom was at the time. Jim had a good job at the post office that he did not want to compromise. The elder Monaghan ran with the business and the younger brother put his energy into other things. When Jim left the business it was hardly worth anything, but Tom gave him a 1959 Volkswagen Beetle that had been used for deliveries.[31]

MAKING SOMETHING OF HIMSELF

Often you see kids with troubled childhoods either recreate the disaster in their adulthood or move away from it. Monaghan was one of those who moved very far away from it. Monaghan became a driven young man. And although his Catholic experiences were not always positive, he developed a strong faith that remains granite tough today. No exaggeration is needed to make Monaghan's faith one for the "books."[32]

Smart in some ways, but not particularly studious, Monaghan's development of Domino's Pizza is one of the greatest success stories in business. His journey to staggering wealth involved a number of trips and falls along the way—often in the early stages due to his work with others who turned out to be unscrupulous or just unsuccessful. At the same time, there were many people he worked with who succeeded along with him.

Monaghan married Margie Zybach while he was struggling to make the business work. She was an excellent partner who helped with his business and had enough patience to put up with the sometimes hot-headed future pizza king. Once the business was in a growth mode, he and his wife made regular trips to view competition and also see the latest equipment that might be used to his competitive advantage. It was during this period that Monaghan developed the seeds of his superior operation that revolutionized the pizza business. Monaghan was a pioneer in pizza delivery in that he made it his focus. He developed high standards for ingredients, packaging, service, and delivery. Equipment that he used reduced waste and helped create consistent quality in every store. He insisted on high standards from his employees.

The Monaghans lived frugally for many years in trailers and invested earnings back into the company. There were many close calls where the business was close to collapse and ruin.

Law suits and bill collection were a part of the Monaghan's existence. Top associates came and went. Disasters occurred. But Monaghan stuck it out. He was not creating a few good stores; he was creating an organization that would spread throughout the country with an appetite for global expansion.

DOMINO EXPANSION

Eventually, Monaghan's efforts paid off. He added some top-notch financial advisors who successfully acquired favorable loans and instituted a first class reporting system that added discipline into the growing operation that kept it on track. The company was expanding in the 1980s, but he slowed it temporarily to take time to fix underperforming stores, make adjustments, and then move ahead.

Once success was on the horizon, Monaghan wanted to build a suitable corporate headquarters for Dominos around Ann Arbor and he envisioned one that architecturally fit into the rural landscape and that would also pay homage to Frank Lloyd Wright. Monaghan hired architect Gunnar Birkerts and together they created the Domino headquarters in what has been suggested is the evolution of Wright's design for today. The Domino Farms property also houses many other offices and buildings—some related to Dominos.

In 1983, Monaghan bought the Detroit Tigers, a team that he had followed and admired. Incredibly, in 1984, the team won the World Series. In 1993, Monaghan sold the Tigers to Mike Ilich, his competitor at Little Caesars Pizza and fellow mega-entrepreneur.

PHILANTHROPY

After 38 years of running Dominos, Monaghan sold controlling interest in the company to Bain Capital. He retains control of Domino Farms. At the time of the sale, Dominos had over 6,000 stores. Since that time, Monaghan has focused on his philanthropic interests. Monaghan was honored with the Pope John Paul II Family Fidelity Award in 1988, the Marine Corps Leatherneck Award in 1990, the Proudly Pro-Life Award in 2000, and the Sports Faith Hall of Fame award in 2010. Whether it's building a chapel at the Domino's headquarters or fighting the government mandate to force organizations to provide birth control coverage in health insurance coverage, Monaghan continues to take a strong stand on issues involving faith. In fact, many would say Monaghan is a crusader for Catholic education and values that many believe were compromised in the last half century.

In 1983, Monaghan created the Ave Maria Foundation to direct his philanthropic efforts in a hands-on way. Every project he supports has his personal stamp of approval on it. Many are huge. What followed was Ave Maria Institute in Ypsilanti that would become Ave Maria College, Ave Maria School of Law, Ave Maria Radio, and the Thomas More Law Center—offering legal aid for people of faith who face religious freedom challenges. Monaghan also created Legatus, an organization of wealthy Catholic business leaders. Monaghan was also the founder and greatest benefactor of Ave Maria University in Florida which was established in 2003. Monaghan, who served as Chief Executive Officer of the university in its early years, currently holds the position of chancellor. Monaghan has also been active in supporting Catholic work and institutions in Nicaragua and Honduras.

Monaghan has received honorary degrees from 12 universities around the country, and in March of 2000, he was named an Honorary Fellow of Magdalene College within Britain's University of Cambridge. Monaghan and his wife, Margie, have four daughters, ten grandchildren, and one great-grandchild.

MARCH FOR LIFE

On January 18, 2015 about 4,000 people walked in the Chicago Loop to proclaim the sanctity of human life and call for the overturn of the 1973 Roe v. Wade decision that legalized abortion in the United States. It was the 10th annual March for Life and drew a diverse collection of citizens from all walks of life and faiths. Included were several politicians and Chicago's Archbishop Blase Cupich. Marchers stopped at the Federal Plaza and the Thompson Center. The author read the poem that follows below:

THE MARCH OF THE PRO-LIFERS[33]
Five cold blocks, five cold blocks
Five cold blocks forward
Through the streets of Chicago
Marched the Pro-Lifers

"Faster, the Pro-Lifers!"
Were we bound for heaven?
As though the marchers knew
Jesus had saved them.
Ours not to march too slow,
Ours not to march for show
Ours but to march and glow
Through the streets of Chicago
Marched the Pro-Lifers.

Encouraged with good spirits,
Faster we marched and well,
Into post march stiffness;
Into the Thompson Center
Marched the Pro-Lifers.

Marched all our reserves bare,
Marched as we needed air
Surging the last block there,
Marching five blocks
Spectators marveled.
Marched through car exhaust smoke
A course record we broke:
We know that life
Begins at conception
After death, heaven

Is a promotion
All the Pro-Lifers

We don't have a palace.
We don't march with malice.
We who had marched so well
Endure post march stiffness
Back at the Thompson Center,
All who started finished
All the Pro-Lifers.

Now will we drink lemonade?
Oh, the strong march we made!
Spectators marveled.
Honor the march we made!
Honor the Brave Marchers-
Noble Pro-Lifers!

— Patrick McCaskey

NEHEMIAH

*O LORD God of heaven, the great and terrible God
who keeps covenant and steadfast love with those
who love him and keep his commandments; let thy
ear be attentive, and thy eyes open, to hear the*

*prayer of thy servant which I now pray before thee
day and night for the people of Israel thy servants,
confessing the sins of the people of Israel, which
we have sinned against thee. Yea, I and my father's
house have sinned. We have acted very corruptly
against thee, and have not kept the commandments,
the statutes, and the ordinances which thou didst
command thy servant Moses. Remember the word
which thou didst command thy servant Moses, saying, 'If you are unfaithful, I will scatter you among
the peoples; but if you return to me and keep my
commandments and do them, though your dispersed
be under the farthest skies, I will gather them thence
and bring them to the place which I have chosen, to
make my name dwell there. They are thy servants
and thy people, whom thou hast redeemed by thy
great power and by thy strong hand. O Lord, let
thy ear be attentive to the prayer of thy servant, and
to the prayer of thy servants who delight to fear thy
name; and give success to thy servant today, and
grant him mercy in the sight of this man.*

— Nehemiah's Prayer, Nehemiah 1:5-11

When I think of perseverance, I think of Nehemiah. In
the fifth century B.C., Nehemiah rebuilt the walls of Jerusalem. It didn't happen all at once, but it happened. After Nehemiah had arrived in Jerusalem, he rested for three days. Then

he said, "Come let us rebuild." Others caught the vision. Still others mocked the re-builders. Nehemiah was prepared for the mockers. He responded in a gentlemanly manner.

Prayer is an excellent preparation. We should pray before we go to the person in authority, the people who will help you, and the people who will mock you.

Nehemiah had three important steps in his prayers. First, he praised God. Then, Nehemiah confessed his sins. Finally, he made his requests.

Nehemiah also analyzed the situation. He inspired others to join the project. He knew that God would provide the necessary strength. He also knew that his opposition wouldn't disappear. To set a good example for his people, he did not profit from the rebuilding of the wall.

Nehemiah received four messages from his opponents for a meeting. He refused to meet with them. He received a fifth message from one of his opponents for a meeting. Nehemiah refused this meeting too. He also denied the rumors of his desire for kingship. He was told to flee, but he refused.

It took fifty-two days to finish the wall.

Nehemiah's people fasted. They wore sackcloth. They covered their heads with dust. They confessed their sins. They read from the book of the law of the Lord. The book was their blueprint for righteous living.

Nehemiah wanted to increase the population of Jerusalem. Perhaps he wanted to make sure there would be enough participation. The walls could have been paid for through fundraisers.

Let us be joyous people. Let us be happy in the Lord. Let us follow the exhortation of Jackie Vernon. He said, "Never spit in another man's face unless his moustache is on fire."

The Ammonites and the Moabites were enemies of Nehemiah's people. In our own day, those who resemble them are denigrators and second-guessers.

When Nehemiah made his final prayers, he mentioned his good works, but he relied on God's mercy.

but they who wait for the Lord shall renew their strength,
they shall mount up with wings like eagles,
they shall run and not be weary,
they shall walk and not faint.

— Isaiah 40:31

GOD'S STRENGTH

For six days a week,
I exercise my gift
Of running.
Even God took a day off.
I was made
In His image.
When I listen
To my body,
I hear the ocean.
When I hold a conch (sea shell)
To my ear,

I hear Eric Liddell run.
On the day
Of rest,
I am God's guest.
His strength renews me.

— Patrick McCaskey

MONK IN THOUGHT AT ST. MICHAEL'S ABBEY
OF THE NORBERTINE FATHERS

FOR THE SAKE OF THE CALL

The Spirit of the Lord is upon me, because he has anointed me to preach good news to the poor. He has sent me to proclaim release to the captives and recovering of sight to the blind, to set at liberty those who are oppressed...

— Luke 4:18

MARTYRS OF KABUL

In 1975, Coach Wayne Gordon moved to North Lawndale on Chicago's Westside. At that time, North Lawndale was one of the poorest neighborhoods in the United States. Gordon was a teacher and coach at Farragut High School—a recent graduate of Wheaton College and a native of Fort Dodge, Iowa. Gordon started the Lawndale Community Church and later with others from the community, he established the Lawndale Christian Development Corporation. The organization was established at a grass roots level with many people from the neighborhood, growing and expanding to new ministries. Rooted in these efforts was an initiative to provide decent health care for the community through the Lawndale Christian Health Center.[34]

Wayne Gordon is a remarkable Pastor, but he prefers to be called, Coach Gordon. Like all great coaches, he has his own coaching tree—others follow his example. But in Coach Gordon's case, they follow him in following Jesus Christ.

Often those who turn their lives over to serve others continue that practice in good times and in bad—in good conditions and in bad conditions. They serve until they can't serve any longer. In some cases, they give up their lives in faithful service of others.

Like Coach Gordon, Dr. Jerry Umanos followed the example of Jesus Christ in service to others. He was one of the original four doctors at the Lawndale Christian Health Center. He spent much of his last seven years in Afghanistan. He worked for CURE International Hospital in Kabul—as a pediatrician caring for children and training Afghan doctors and nurses. In that time, he not only helped his Afghan patients, but he also helped prepare others to continue after him.

The Gabel family belonged to the Orchard Evangelical Free Church in Arlington Heights, Illinois. Gary Gabel sang in the church choir and was involved with the church youth groups and the leadership team. His son, John Gabel, played center on the church basketball team.

John Gabel was a colleague and friend of Dr. Umanos. Working for the U.S.-based charity Morning Star Development, John ran a health clinic at Kabul University and taught computer science classes. The clinic provided pharmacy and emergency care for the students, professors, and employees. Beth Anderson, a family friend, said John Gabel was "greatly affected" by the September 11 attacks and war in Afghanistan.

He "kept caring long after it seemed the rest of us lost touch with what was going on there."[35]

Gary Gabel was proud of the work his son was doing in Afghanistan and he and his wife went to visit his son. On April 24, 2014, a security guard assigned to the CURE International Hospital in Kabul shot and killed Dr. Umanos and John and Gary Gabel in cold blood. John Gabel's wife, Teresa, was wounded. The shooter sustained self-inflicted injuries and was treated by the doctors on staff before being taken away by Afghan authorities. The death of these men will be felt by their families, church communities, and thousands of Afghans who were helped by Dr. Jerry and John Gabel.

Dr. Umanos wife, Jan Schuitema, described her husband's faith and his work in Afghanistan:

> *"He always had a desire to be the hands and feet of Christ. He was always a light for Christ and he had a love and commitment that he expressed for the Afghan people because of that love for Christ."*

SAINT MICHAEL'S ABBEY

The Norbertine Order of the Catholic Church was founded in France in 1121, by Saint Norbert, an affluent man who acquired a position in the church that provided a comfortable living and little sacrifice. It was not good enough. Norbert experienced a moral awakening, which came to a head when he rode his horse to a nearby village. A thunderbolt struck at his horse's feet and like Saint Paul, he was thrown to the ground and injured. After recovering, Norbert committed himself to Jesus and rid himself of all his possessions. He received the pope's permission to become a missionary preacher. He roamed through lands that are now Germany, Belgium, and France—preaching repentance and reform. On Christmas day, 1120, Norbert established a religious order committed to seek Christ by means of active ministry, community living, poverty, obedience, and celibacy. His Norbertine Order has grown and spread out to other parts of the world.

In 1950, around 2,500 monks and nuns were deported from Hungary by the Communist regime. Seven Hungarian refugees from the Norbertine Abbey of Saint Michael at Csorna fled their country and made their way to the United States.[36] They purchased property in Orange County California and opened Saint Michael's Junior Seminary and Novitiate in September of 1961. The monastic community they built attracted many in the 1960s. During this time of social upheaval numerous men joined the group, but few stayed. The Norbertine Monks fortified their community by taking a strong position to remain loyal to the Church and the authority of the Holy Father. They established a policy "not to reject what is good in the old, and to take what is good in the new."[37] They sought like-minded young men to enter the community and the community grew healthy.

In 1976, Saint Michael's became fully autonomous as an independent priory of the Order and in 1984, the community was elevated to abbatial status. In 1996, the abbey established a foundation for cloistered, contemplative women in Tehachapi. The priests of the abbey provide daily pastoral care for the sisters in Tehachapi, which has grown from very humble beginnings to an abbey with enough land and facilities to develop self-sufficiency.

Saint Michael's Abbey is an autonomous abbey of the Norbertine Order that currently has 49 solemnly professed members, and 25 seminarians studying for the priesthood. The abbey's principal apostolate is its school, Saint Michael's Preparatory School. Members of the Abbey also provide Sunday ministry at over 30 parishes and institutions. They teach at all levels of schools from elementary to college. Priests give retreats to many different religious communities including a community of Rosarian Dominican Sisters who maintained a convent at the abbey. The Abbey also assists in many Catholic organizations, offers prison ministry, and staffing of parishes. Spiritual direction and counseling; sacramental care to the dying; and assistance to Catholic cemeteries is also provided. The seminarians' time of formation before ordination is at least ten years for those who enter the community with a bachelor's degree, and proportionately longer for younger men.

After more than 50 years in the same rural Trabuco Canyon location, the Norbertine Fathers of St. Michael's Abbey purchased 320 acres in Silverado Canyon to which they plan to relocate their Abbey. Grading work has begun.[38]

PRESS ON

I press on toward the goal for the prize of the upward call of God in Christ Jesus.

— *Philippians 3:14*

God created
electricity, cotton, and many other wonders.
Benjamin Franklin discovered electricity.
Someone might have said to him,
"Go fly a kite."
Eli Whitney invented the cotton gin.
I am allergic to synthetics,
but God, Franklin, and Whitney
fortify me.
When it comes to ironing cotton handkerchiefs,
I press on.
Take nothing for granted.
Work like a dog
with a cheerful attitude.
Train diligently.
Leave the results to God.
John Cassis says,
"Concentrate on the gold,
not on all the dirt."
Saint Paul says,
"Press on."
While you press on,
keep your eyes fixed
upon the Lord.

— Patrick McCaskey

Brother Matthew Desme

Grant Desme was born April 4, 1986 in Bakersfield, California. His love of baseball blossomed as a student at Stockdale High. He was first team selectee for the Southwest Yosemite League. As a senior, he was named Co-MVP of the League. In college, he earned the title of Big West Conference Player of the Year at California Polytechnic State University, San Luis Obispo.

Grant got his start in his professional career with the Short-Season Vancouver Canadians of the Northwest League of Professional Baseball in 2007. He batted .261 with three doubles, one home run, six RBIs, and two stolen bases. In the 2008 season, he only played in two games after he was injured. Then in 2009 he hit a combined .288 with 31 doubles, 6 triples, 31 home runs, 89 RBIs and 40 stolen bases in 131 games for the Class-A Kane County Cougars and the Class-A Advanced Stockton Ports. The Arizona Fall League's Joe Black Most Valuable Player Award followed these achievements!

Desme discerned his Priesthood vocation during rehabilitation time. He spent time in silence and solitude during this period that caused him to think beyond his baseball career. He thought about how he might be judged as a disciple of Christ and determined that he needed a deeper more prayerful relationship with God.

When Desme considered the priesthood, his vocation followed naturally. He felt called and offered no opposition. But after his injury recovery, he came back to baseball for one more year and played some of his best baseball. He left after he had proven himself. Most in baseball believe he would have become a starter if not a star had he continued to play. Desme shocked the baseball world on January 22, 2010 when he announced plans to retire from professional baseball and begin his studies to become a Roman Catholic priest.

Desme Sees Other Options for Young Men

"I was doing well at baseball. But I really had to get down to the bottom of things—I love the game but I aspire to higher things. I wasn't at peace where I was at. I have no regrets. In retrospect, those injuries were the biggest blessings God ever gave me."

Desme left behind his baseball contract, shiny SUV and other worldly trappings to embrace a life of poverty, celibacy, and obedience at Saint Michael's Abbey. Today, he is called Brother (Frater) Matthew. He has several more years of study before he becomes a priest.

"I would recommend looking into the priesthood to young men who think they might be called. There's nothing the world needs more than the mercy of Jesus Christ, which is granted through his priests. It's a spiritual fatherhood that is even more profound than physical fatherhood. It's something the saints have written about in almost unbelievable terms. It's mind-boggling to think of what Jesus wants to give us through spiritual fathers."[39]

Desme, like Father Joe Freedy,[40] the University of Buffalo quarterback who became a priest, thought about the meaning of masculinity. For Desme, real masculinity is based on self-sacrificing love.

> *"Being a man is not about stepping on others, but lifting others up. It's about using the God-given strength you have to protect others and guide them to eternal life."[41]*

Desme suggests that real Christianity calls for toughness and that when we attempt to live it out, it requires a complete dedication. He describes his life at the abbey as a challenging one, "which is about dying to self in order to live for Jesus."[42]

For most young men, it's hard to imagine giving up a major league career for the priesthood. But it was really a clear choice for Grant Desme.

> *"It's a miracle in a way. It's so abnormal to give something up that you've been working for your whole life, that millions of kids growing up around the country would want. To walk away from it, it's like, 'What's going on?' It's the working of God's grace and love. That's the only way it happens. I thought about it afterward. There are tons of minor league players, big leaguers, who get hurt. None of them reacted this way. For whatever reason, God chose me."[43]*

Desme's new life requires the greatest sacrifice, dying to self—leaving what he wanted behind and following God's will. He now lives in God's house, where Jesus dwells.

Perhaps more than anything, Desme is focused on God's will:

"The only thing that will last after death is our relationship—or lack thereof — with God. This is something that should motivate everyone to see past the superficial things of life that clamor for our attention and instead invest our lives in God, trusting in his mercy."

Sports Faith International honored Grant Desme with the Father Smyth Award in 2011 that goes to an exceptional athlete who leaves behind a promising career in sports for a religious vocation.

Joshua's Advice

Have I not commanded you? Be strong and of good courage; be not frightened, neither be dismayed; for the Lord your God is with you wherever you go.
— Joshua 1:9

BE STRONG AND COURAGEOUS
Run the mile,
With a smile.
Then idle awhile.
Read the Bible.
If you read inside,
Open the door

Before you try
To run some more.
God is with you
Wherever you go.
Don't go slow.
Use the talents
That God gave you.
If you fall,
Don't feel small
Unless you are.
Regardless of your size,
Be strong and courageous,
Not wrong and outrageous.

— Patrick McCaskey

FATHER MASTERS

Some people believe sports can be a barrier to faith; at best a distraction, at its worst, a kind of false god that young people can worship. But over and over again in my life and work, sports and faith continue to coexist in positive ways. Father Burke Masters's story illustrates this.

Father Burke Masters was born and raised in Joliet, Illinois, the youngest of three sons of Tod and Janet Masters. His parents were raised as members of Christian churches and although they remained believers in Jesus

Christ, as adults they were neither involved in church nor did they attend.

Like many other boys, young Burke wanted to become a Major League baseball player. He was attracted to Providence Catholic High School in New Lenox, Illinois, because of its academic and athletic programs that could help him go on to college. It must have been odd for the young man with no formal religious background to walk the halls at Providence and see priests and nuns. Theology classes received his attention and interest. He was drawn to Jesus.

> *"Sr. Margaret Anne gave me my first Bible and encouraged me to read it, starting with the Gospel of Matthew. As I began to read the Bible, my heart began to fill with a peace and joy that I had never experienced before. It reminds me of what St. Augustine once said, 'My heart is restless until it rests in thee.' And my heart had been restless, but Christ was changing it little by little. I was also very intrigued by the Catholic teaching of the Eucharist. How could Jesus be truly present in bread and wine?"*

Masters began to attend Mass, but as a non-Catholic, he did not receive Communion. One day at a lightly attended Mass with worshippers gathered around the altar, the priest stepped forward to give out Communion. He placed the Eucharist on Masters' tongue just as the young man was opening his mouth to tell him that he was not a Catholic.

BURKE MASTERS, SEC SCHOLAR-ATHLETE OF THE YEAR

"At that moment I felt the most powerful presence of Jesus in my body that I had ever felt until that point. I remember thinking, 'Now I understand what they have been trying to teach me.' I began to believe in the Real Presence of Christ in the Eucharist. It was this desire to receive the Eucharist as often as possible that spurred me to join the Catholic Church."

On May 26, 1985, Masters was baptized, received his second Communion, and was confirmed.

After graduation, Masters attended Mississippi State University where he was both an exceptional student and baseball player. Masters is remembered for his performance in a single game that for Mississippi State fans is one of the greatest sports highlights in the school's history. It was 1990, and Mississippi State was down 8–7 against Florida State in the South Regional. Burke Masters was 5-for-5 for the Bulldogs in the game as he stepped up to the plate with bases loaded. On a 3-1 count, Masters smashed a home run to left to win the game. The drama and thrill of victory is remembered to this day by Mississippi State fans. Masters story from the baseball diamond to the priesthood was also highlighted in a John Grisham narration SEC 75: A Story of Character film clip created to celebrate the conference's 75-year history.

While Masters was attending Mississippi State, he visited many churches of his friends. The preaching and the music were inspiring, but his thoughts and his heart fell back on the Eucharist. He found himself at home at Mass.

Although his college baseball career was successful and his team played in the College World Series, he was not drafted by Major League Baseball. For a short time, he worked as an actuarial analyst for Kemper Insurance. In order to get back to baseball, he earned a master's degree in Sports Administration from Ohio University, which he thought could lead to a General Manager position. After he finished his studies, he began to work for the Kane County Cougars in

Geneva, Illinois. He enjoyed the work, but he found himself being pulled toward the priesthood. He entered Mundelein Seminary in 1997 and he was ordained to the priesthood for the Diocese of Joliet in June of 2002. After 4 years at St. Mary's in West Chicago, he became the Vocation Director for the Diocese of Joliet.

Father Masters has also been involved in "Spirit and Truth," a young adult Eucharistic Adoration community program that has gatherings that include a talk, adoration, and then fellowship time. The program has brought young adults of like minds together, fostered vocations, and also brought together people who have gotten married. There are three groups now in the Diocese of Joliet.

Father Masters is also the Chaplain for the Chicago Cubs. He has a popular blog on which he posts his reflections on the daily readings that is followed by people from dozens of countries. Father Masters received Sports Faith International's Father Smyth Award that recognizes an athlete who has left the sports world for a religious vocation.

CARDINAL GEORGE

His Eminence Francis Eugene Cardinal George was born in Chicago to Francis J. and Julia R. McCarthy George on January 16, 1937. He attended Saint Pascal Grade School on Chicago's northwest side and Saint Henry Preparatory Seminary in Belleville, Illinois. After a five-month bout with polio at age 13, he was left with permanent damage to his legs.

He entered the Missionary Oblates of Mary Immaculate in 1957. After studying theology at the University of Ottawa, Canada, he was ordained a priest in 1963 at Saint Pascal Church.

Cardinal George earned a master's degree in Philosophy, a master's degree in Theology, a doctorate in American Philosophy, and a doctorate of Sacred Theology. He taught at several seminaries and universities. For the Missionary Oblates of Mary Immaculate, he was Provincial Superior of the Midwestern Province and was then elected Vicar General of the Oblates and served in Rome from 1974-1986. The nearly 4,000 Missionary Oblates serve those most in need in some of the world's most difficult missions.

They are comfort to the sick, food to the hungry and hope for the orphaned. They bring peace to war-torn nations and spiritual healing to people in need.[44]

Pope Saint John Paul II appointed George to be Bishop of Yakima where he served for five and a half years before being appointed Archbishop of Portland by the Pope in 1996. In 1997, Pope Saint John Paul II named him the eighth Archbishop of Chicago to replace Joseph Cardinal Bernardin who had died in 1996.

On January 18, 1998, Pope Saint John Paul II announced Archbishop George's elevation to the Sacred College of Cardinals. He was appointed by Pope Saint John Paul II and Pope Benedict XVI to dozens of important committees and initiatives of the Catholic Church. He holds many other memberships in boards and other groups.

Cardinal George was publisher of The Catholic New World and Chicago Católico newspapers of the Archdiocese of Chicago. He has written books, pastoral letters, newspaper columns and much more. In addition to English, he speaks French, Italian, Spanish, and some German.

Breakfast with the Cardinal

In the year 2000, I sent a collection of my poems to Cardinal George because he has a very difficult job and I wanted to give him some respectful comic relief. In 2004, my mother was invited to have breakfast with Cardinal George at his home, and she asked me to go with her. During breakfast, Cardinal George asked me a deep theological question.

"Will you please pass me the orange juice?"

After I had passed him the orange juice, he asked me, "Isn't it unusual for a sportsman to write poetry?"

I replied, "First of all, it's a gift."

Cardinal George said, "I understand that."

I said, "Yes, it's unusual."

Cardinal George's Books

Cardinal George and I have several things in common. He was born in Illinois. So was I. He was an altar boy. So was I. His first name is Francis. I was born in Saint Francis Hospital. When someone asks me, "How do you find time to write books?" My humorous response is "during the bye week." My serious response is "Cardinal George is busier than I am and he writes excellent books." In his book "God in Action: How Faith in God Can Address the Challenges of the World," Cardinal George calls on us to "rely on and cooperate with the providence of God." I not only read Cardinal George's books, I buy them. When I read Cardinal George's book, "The Difference God Makes," I heard Dinah Washington sing "What a Difference a Day Makes" and I rewrote the lyrics into a poem.

What a difference that God makes
He has almighty powers
Made the sun and the flowers
He also provides rain

My yesterday was blue, God
Today I'm part of you, God
My lonely nights are through, God
Since we have been entwined

What a difference that God makes
There's a rainbow before me
Even when skies are stormy
We have the Cardinal's book, that well-written book

It's heaven when you find mercy on your menu
What a difference that God makes
And the difference is grace.

— Patrick McCaskey

Cardinal George is a learned man known for humility and a pragmatic, faithful approach to his ministry. Cardinal George retired in 2014 and he was replaced by Bishop Blase Cupich.

FATHER LIGHTNER

It is our vocation and a privilege to be the arms, feet, eyes, ears and voice of Christ in the world. Joined with our fellow members, we really do make a difference, and our lives are blessed many times over. May we always be one in the Spirit!

— Father Mike Lightner

Father Mike Lightner was born on the feast of Saint Francis of Assisi. Lightner comes from an athletic family in Oconto, Wisconsin, north of Green Bay. As a standout athlete in high school, he accepted a full scholarship to play football at the University of Eastern Michigan. At 6 foot 4 and 330 pounds, he was an ideal candidate for an NFL offensive lineman. On a pilgrimage to Madjugorje, with his mother Joyce, the Lord called to Mike to play for His team. Through his incredible confession, to seeing God's Healing Power first-hand, this college football-player was deeply moved by God's Divine Mercy.

Father Lightner earned a Masters in Divinity from Mount Saint Mary's University in Emmitsburg, Maryland. He was ordained a priest on May 21, 2005, by Timothy Cardinal Dolan who served as the Archbishop of Milwaukee at the time.

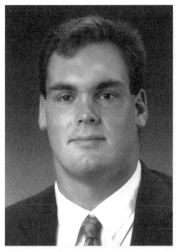

MICHAEL LIGHTNER AS STUDENT

After his ordination, Father Lightner was appointed Associate Pastor of Saint Francis Borgia in Cedarburg, Wisconsin. Today, he is the Director of Apostolate of Prayer in the Archdiocese of Milwaukee, and Parish Administrator of St. Margaret Mary in Milwaukee. On February 23, 2014, Sports Faith International awarded Father Michael Lightner the 2014 Fr. John Smyth Award that recognizes an outstanding Catholic athlete or coach who pursues a religious vocation.

POPE SAINT JOHN PAUL II

He was born in Wadowice, Poland.
He visited 129 countries.
He spoke 14 languages fluently.
He had a 27-year papacy.

When he played soccer, he was a goalie.
He was a great sport and very holy.
He was a volunteer librarian.
He wrote very well, a grammarian.

An actor, a playwright, and a poet,
When he was hiding, foes didn't know it.
A laborer in a limestone quarry,
He also did work in a factory.

Priest, bishop, archbishop, cardinal, pope,
He served God Almighty, he did not mope.
An ethics teacher with two doctorates,
He was surely one of the all-time greats.

A hiker, a jogger, a kayaker,
A skier, a swimmer, a weight lifter,
After a 1981 attempt
To assassinate him, he was resilient.

A camper, an editor, a speaker,
Pope Saint John Paul II wrote 14 encyclicals.
He worked to end many a Church schism.
He was also tough on Communism.

Venerable, beatified, saintly,
Pope Saint John Paul II had heroic virtues.

— Patrick McCaskey

BILL DANA AND DANNY THOMAS

WE ARE HUMBLED

Many are the plans in the mind of a man, but it is the purpose of the Lord that will be established.
— *Proverbs 19:21*

Everyone needs a sense of humor. It's difficult to say whether or not we humans are naturally logical thinkers. Most people believe that we develop common sense that helps us get through most days without a series of catastrophes. But the moment we start thinking that we have all the answers, we are usually humbled by our Creator. The cycle of learning the ropes and then finding that the ropes don't quite hold, is something that tests our sense of humor.

SZATHMARY TO DANA TO JIMENEZ

My mom and dad appreciated humor and they certainly needed it while raising 11 McCaskey children. And like my parents, I enjoy it myself, but it can sometimes be difficult to find the wholesome variety on television. One of my parents' favorite comedians was Bill Dana. Dana had his own program, "The Bill Dana Show," from 1963 to 1965 and it was rerun on the Christian Broadcasting Network (CBN) in glorious black and white in the 1980s.

Dana's real name is William Szathmary; he was born in Quincy, Massachusetts, on October 5, 1924. Dana's father, who came from Hungary at the age of 14, did real estate work until the stock market crash in 1929. Dana never knew luxury; in fact, when he went into the service during World War II, he couldn't believe he was receiving free food.

Dana was the youngest of six (he had four brothers and one sister). While a student at Daniel Webster Grammar School, his teacher said to him one day, "Szathmary, you're a buffoon." He replied, "Let's keep religion out of this."

The Szathmary family was fairly ecumenical. They were Jewish, but were raised with Catholics. Dana knew the Stations of the Cross, and he used his knowledge of Catholicism in his humor:

> *"During the ceremony where novitiates become Brides of Christ (Religious Sisters), the bishop noticed an Orthodox Jewish man praying loudly. Not being able to conquer his curiosity, the bishop had to stop the ceremony long enough to ask the man, 'Sir, I realize you are not a Catholic. I must ask you why you are here at this marriage of our Lord to these novitiates?'" The old man answered with a lovely, Jewish accent, 'I'm on the groom's side.'"*
>
> *— Bill Dana*

After graduation from Quincy High School, Dana went into the Army Air Corps and then the infantry. He served a little over three years during World War II (1942-1945). He was decorated for "extreme precaution under cover."

Dana, who describes himself as a Jewish dropout because he doesn't have a PhD, went to Emerson College in Boston on the GI Bill. He graduated with high honors in speech and drama, and had a minor in English. He and a friend built the campus radio station, WERS.

He initially couldn't get a job out of college, but by a fluke, he eventually landed a job with the Douglas Testing Division in Santa Monica, California, on the Nike Project (the code name for an anti-aircraft missile system that was being developed by the United States). A friend of Dana's, Gene Wood, happened to be a page at NBC in New York, so Dana decided to take a leave from Douglas to see his friend. He never returned to Douglas, and the rest, as they say, is history!

Dana wrote the material that got a young comedian named Don Adams (who later starred in the 1960s TV series "Get Smart") on "The Steve Allen Show" during the 1950s and 1960s. He became the head writer for the show, but also served as a very popular member of the ensemble playing his alter ego, Jose Jimenez. Dana was a guest on many television programs.

Neil Simon, a staff member on "The Garry Moore Show," asked Jose Jimenez if he had ever been an astronaut and immediately, Jose Jimenez "the reluctant astronaut," was born. At the inaugural gala of President John F. Kennedy in 1961, Dana teamed up with Milton Berle for a routine called, "Jose the Astronaut." Interestingly, Dana became the honorary eighth astronaut in the Mercury space program—the program that put the first American astronauts in space (there were seven Mercury astronauts). On May 5, 1961, the first words from the ground to Alan Shepard—the first American in space—were, "OK, Jose, you're on your way."

Dana went on to write the most popular half-hour episode in the history of the Television—"Sammy Davis Visits the Bunkers"—in 1972 for "All in the Family." Some kind of clerical error prevented what many deemed to be a shoe in for an Emmy. At the same time the movie, "Brian's Song," about Brian Piccolo and the Bears, won several awards that year. Years later, Dana entertained at the Brian Piccolo Golf Tournament Banquet "to get revenge." He asked for and received a standing ovation.

Dana entertained at my parents' 40th wedding anniversary party on February 6, 1983. In recent years, he has done a lot of work on the healing power of laughter. In his book *The Laughter Prescription,* Dana states:

> *"Stress is connected with all of man's physical problems. If you have cancer, just tell it a good joke: Titters for the terminal. Anybody in a survival mode has to have humor or it's over and out."*

BEHAVE LIKE CHAMPIONS

When I was a child, there was a series of books called "Vision Books." They were about saints and other wonderful people. My mother gave us these books for ourselves and for our friends when we were invited to their birthday parties.

My two favorite books in this series were "Champions in Sports and Spirit" and "More Champions in Sports and Spirit."

The first book was about Yogi Berra (baseball), Terry Brennan (football), Maureen Connolly (tennis), Bob Cousy (basketball), Gil Hodges (baseball), Rocky Marciano (boxing), and Maurice Richard (hockey). The second book was about Eddie Arcaro (horseracing), Carmen Basilio (boxing), Jean Beliveau (hockey), Ron Delany (track), Juan Manuel Fangio (auto racing), Stan Musial (baseball), Alex Olmedo (tennis), and Herb Score (baseball).

Regardless of what happens on the field, let's behave like champions in sports and spirit. Let's not analyze. Let's not denigrate. Let's not second guess. Let's not diagnose injuries before we've read the x-rays. Let sportsmanship prevail. John Wooden used to say, "Win with humility. Lose with grace."

Chip off the Old Block

Another book series that I enjoyed as a child was the Chip Hilton series written by Clair Bee, a Hall of Fame basketball coach. Chip was a great sport and near perfect in many ways. He always helped his teammates improve their game and their values. He was one of my heroes and I suppose still is today.

In Book 12 of the Chip Hilton Sports Series, "Ten Seconds to Play," Coach Ralston evaluates Chip:

> *"Once in a long time, once in a blue moon, a player comes along with the spark of greatness which can mean the difference between a mediocre team and a great one. This spark of greatness or spirit or soul or genius—call it what you wish—is a combination of wisdom, leadership, intuition, loyalty, and unwavering courage."*

THE SPIRIT OF CHIP HILTON

One day
My wife gave me a list
of things to do.
I asked her,
"Who do you think I am,
Chip Hilton?"
She replied,
"You're my Chip Hilton."
I completed the list
and some more besides.
A victory is like kissing your wife.

— Patrick McCaskey

RICH DONNELLY

Rich Donnelly is a baseball-lifer who continues to pace base-ball diamonds into his late 60s. He is also a devout Catholic who as a young man once entertained dreams of being a Catholic priest. In Donnelly's case, humor was the pathway for special communication.

Donnelly's most recent assignment is Seattle Mariner third base coach. He's been around the block in his 40 plus years in baseball. He was a major league coach for the Rangers, Marlins, Brewers, Dodgers, Rockies, and Pirates, as well as a minor league player and manager. He is also known as a man of God in large part because of how the truly remarkable story of his daughter Amy affected his faith.[45]

As third base coach for the Pittsburgh Pirates in 1992, Donnelly would crouch down, cup his hands, and shout instructions to the runner on second base. His daughter, Amy, once teased him:

> *"Dad, what are you yelling to the runner, 'The chicken runs at midnight?'"*

Although the statement had no real meaning, it caught on as a catch phrase in the Donnelly home and at the ballpark by the Pirates. It was caught on microphone when Pittsburgh second baseman Jose Lind ran on the field before a game in 1992 yelling to teammates, "Let's go, the chicken runs at midnight!"

Amy Donnelly was diagnosed with a brain tumor in spring training 1992. She died nine months later at age 18.[46] Four years later, Donnelly was coaching the Marlins in Game 7 of the World Series at Dolphin Stadium. In the 11th inning, Donnelly waved home Craig Counsell for the winning run. Counsell was nicknamed "The Chicken" in the Donnelly house because he flapped his left elbow as he got ready for the pitch to be delivered. As Counsell crossed the plate, the crowd roared, but time stood still for the Donnelly's. Tim Donnelly, one of Amy's younger brothers, looked at the clock and screamed to his brother, and fellow bat boy Mike to do the same. Then they screamed to their dad, Rich Donnelly, "Dad, look at the time! Look at the time!" Donnelly glanced up, it was midnight. *The chicken runs at midnight.*

Donnelly firmly believes that Amy was sending him a message from Heaven, and this experience has solidified his faith in God even more.

BOB THOMAS

BOB THOMAS

Bob Thomas was a kicker who played 12 seasons in the NFL. He was drafted by the Rams in the late rounds of the 1974 draft. The Bears picked him up and he spent most of his career in Chicago where he became the Bears all-time leading scorer. He was a steady kicker for the Bears and towards the end of his career after he was released, he moved on to San Diego in 1985 and played briefly for the Giants in 1986.

Bear fans remember Thomas's yeoman service. In 1977, after a long absence from the post-season, the Bears faced the Giants in the last game of the season. They needed a win to make the playoffs. Walter Payton was having a phenomenal year—for the season he would be the league's leading rusher, the leader in rushing touchdowns, the leader in yards from scrimmage, and several other marks. But as football fans know, often the whole season comes down to one kick. Thomas hit a 28 yard field goal in overtime to win the game.

Thomas was born in Rochester, New York. He attended McQuaid Jesuit High School where he played both football and soccer while excelling academically. Boys of all faiths are accepted at McQuaid. Jesuit principles are promoted:

In the Jesuit tradition, there is no life without learning, no learning without love, and no love without God. Everything at McQuaid Jesuit is based on this belief. McQuaid Jesuit students are invited—indeed challenged—to become "Men for Others," dedicated to serving God and humanity and guided by a profound sense of justice.[47]

Thomas went on to Notre Dame. His Sugar Bowl performance on December 31, 1973 is still remembered with great fondness. Paul "Bear" Bryant and Alabama met Ara Parseghian and Notre Dame for what was essentially the national championship. Thomas's 19-yard field goal in the fourth quarter won the game for the Irish.

While on the Bears, Thomas attended Loyola University School of Law and received his J.D. in 1981. Thomas practiced law and became a judge. He served in several judicial capacities including Illinois Supreme Court Chief Justice from 2005-2008. Today, he still serves on the Illinois Supreme Court. Thomas was inducted into the Academic All-American Hall of Fame in 1996, he received the NCAA Silver Anniversary Award in 1999, and he was inducted into the Chicagoland Sports Hall of Fame.

Thomas has been a strong advocate for fairness and spoke about the need for collegiality and professional civility in the legal profession. In his first remarks as Chief Justice, he said:

"As lawyers and judges, we must remember one essential fact: At the heart of every case is a human being—a person for whom this particular case means everything." [48]

Central to Bob Thomas is His Faith

My faith is very important to me. I have been blessed with two great careers. Knowing that self-esteem is not based on what you do but rather that you are a child of God becomes the most important factor in my personal life. [49]

— *Bob Thomas*

Thomas wrote a book with Gregg Lewis called *Good Sports: Making Sports a Positive Experience for Everyone* published by Zondervan Publishing House. In *Good Sports*,

Thomas recalls how he was influenced by his "old world" soc-
cer-playing dad, he remembers his own soccer career that led
him to the NFL, and then he takes a hard look at youth sports
today. As a father, Thomas examines where sports might go if
indeed we really want it to work for kids. Only a judge and a
professional athlete could provide such insights!

According to Thomas, as a Christian he sees many things in
sports that run contrary to Jesus's life of servitude and to a Christian's responsibilities. For Thomas, today's playing fields promote
many values that most of us do not want our children to follow.
Are youth sports concerned with helping produce professional
athletes or do they produce happy healthy well rounded kids?
Thomas suggests that we take a hard look at our overemphasis on
winning, unrealistic demands, and inappropriate adult behavior.

Finally, Thomas suggests that we help our kids look at role
models from professional sports. As our kids look out on the
world of profession sports, do they understand that the role models they look up to one minute can fall to temptation the next?

SHAKESPEARE AT HALFTIME[50]

One more half to play for the victory,
And end the game with our best effort!
In church there's nothing so becoming
As modest stillness and humility,
But when the whistle blows to restart the game,
Then imitate the action of Bears:
Stiffen the sinews, summon up the blood,

Disguise fair nature with hard-favored rage;
Then lend the eye a terrible aspect:
Let it pry through the portage of the head
Like the brass cannon; let the brow overwhelm it
As fearfully as does a galled rock
Overhang and jutty his confounded base,
Swilled with the wild and wasteful ocean.
Now set the teeth and stretch the nostril wide,
Hold hard the breath and bend up every spirit
To its full height! Go, go you great Bears,
Whose blood is full from fathers of game-proof,
Fathers that like so many coaches
Have in these parts from morn till even played
And then stopped playing for lack of games.
Dishonor not your mothers; now play hard
That those whom you called fathers did beget you!
Be copy now to men of grosser blood
And teach them how to play! And you, good coaches,
Whose limbs were made quite near here, show us here
The mettle of your coaching. Let us pledge
That you are worth your breeding; which I doubt not,
For there is none of you so mean and base
That has not noble luster in your eyes.
I see you, Bears, ready to play,
Straining for the kickoff. The game's today!
Follow your spirit; and upon this charge
Cry "God for our coaches and the Chicago Bears!"

— Patrick McCaskey

A Journey to Faith

For I am already on the point of being sacrificed; the time of my departure has come. I have fought the good fight, I have finished the race, I have kept the faith. Henceforth there is laid up for me the crown of righteousness, which the Lord, the righteous judge, will award to me on that Day, and not only to me but also to all who have loved his appearing.

— 2 Timothy 4:6-8

Bob Ladouceur Stands Tall

Winning is every football coach's key objective, but Bob Ladouceur focuses on team building, creating a brotherhood among his players, and getting a commitment from each player to put aside his own ego and work for the greater good. If his program sounds like Christian thinking—well Coach Ladouceur also teaches religious studies. For Ladouceur, he does not want to just win, but he wants to win as a team.

In 1979, a 25-year old Ladouceur began coaching the De La Salle Spartans in Concord, California. He had no coaching experience and he took over a team that had never enjoyed a winning season since the school's founding in 1965.

Ladouceur is an intense introvert who taps into the adolescent mind. He teaches and gives his players the opportunity to develop life skills; he encourages them to respect each other; and he takes it one step further—he expects his players to love one another. They demonstrate their love by their contributions to the team. Each player makes a commitment to meet his responsibilities. Each player improves physically, spiritually, and emotionally.

According to Ladouceur:

> *I am a good teammate or team player simply means I know how to sacrifice for a just cause, cooperate with my fellow human, respect the dignity of others, and can respond when called upon.*

Ladouceur keeps things simple. He cannot concentrate on the game when he wears a headset, so he doesn't use them. He uses plays that work with his team's strengths and limits the number of plays to avoid confusion. His weight room has no music—it's a place for work. He believes a head coach must understand each position and coach every minute during practice and games. He believes in goal setting, consistent discipline, and honest dealing with his players. He works hard to improve technique.

Ladouceur's high school record is off the charts. He stepped down from head coach to assistant at the beginning of 2013. Over the 34 years he served as head coach, Ladouceur's De La Salle Spartans were 399–25–3. His teams had 20 undefeated seasons and during one amazing period from 1992 to 2003, Ladouceur's Spartans had a 151-game winning streak without a loss.

Ladouceur was honored as Sports Faith International's Coach of the Year in 2010, he was enshrined into the National High School Hall of Fame in 2001, and he has a trophy case of other awards. Although there is no high school national champion, media sources have named his De La Salle teams the best in the nation six times.[51]

Neil Hayes, now a columnist for the *Chicago Sun-Times* wrote *When the Game Stands Tall*, a book based on Ladouceur's De La Salle teams. The book has also been made into a movie of the same name, directed by Thomas Carter with actor Jim Caviezel playing Ladouceur.

De La Salle's Frank Allocco

Frank Allocco was born and raised in New Providence, New Jersey. He attended New Providence High School where he was all-state in football, basketball, and baseball. He was the Scholar Athlete for the class of 1971. Then he played football and basketball for the University of Notre Dame.

But Allocco's athletic career was not all success. While still a young man in high school he asked his coach, Don Carpenter, to teach him drills that could lead him to become starting quarterback at Notre Dame. It seemed an unreachable goal for a boy who was undersized. But Allocco was not deterred. He practiced and he grew stronger. In his junior year, he started getting noticed by many colleges. But early in his senior year, he broke his collar bone. He was helped by Sister John Betrams, a family friend who reminded him that in his sorrows he walks with Christ. He focused on basketball and after a visit by Notre Dame's assistant Joe Yonto, he received a football scholarship. At Notre Dame, he was way down a long list of quarterbacks. He worked his way up through the ranks, but in his senior year, he was injured again. He decided to come back for another year, but his recovery fell short. He played in several key games for the fighting Irish, but essentially his dreams were unfulfilled. Disappointed, Allocco finally realized his goals were not God's plan for him. But he had learned much about sports that he could teach others. There was much that Allocco could do to help young men succeed in sports and faith.[52]

FRANK ALLOCCO OF DE LA SALLE HIGH SCHOOL

In 1976, Allocco moved to California where he served as athletic director and coach in the Catholic Youth Organization. In 1981, he founded Excel in Basketball summer camps. In 1991, Allocco became the head basketball coach at Northgate High School in California. They won the state championship in 1995. In 1997, Frank became the head basketball coach at De La Salle High School in Concord, California. They won the state championship in 2000 and 2006. He continues teaching, coaching, and reaching out to young athletes in many ways. In 2014, Allocco was named to coach McDonald's All-American West Team.

Allocco is an intense, foot stomping, detail-minded coach who is constantly teaching from his deep knowledge of the game—making the most of his talent to communicate with young men about sports and life.

According to Bob Ladouceur:

"Frank is a very devout Catholic who is active in youth sports and community. He sees his coaching career as a vocation. He uses basketball as a vehicle to move kids to see the bigger picture beyond themselves. He teaches his kids to be servants to their fellow man. From the court to his chapel services he instills all the intangibles in his players of what it means to be an authentic teammate. These intangibles serve his students well beyond their playing days. This is evidenced by how many of his players become teachers and coaches themselves.

They start, while playing for him, by coaching and refereeing in his summer camps and CYO Leagues. Frank volunteers his time organizing and administrating in CYO leagues."

According to the president of the Diablo East CYO, Jack McDonough:

"I have always found Frank Allocco to be a man of tremendously high ethical and moral values. It can be seen in the manner in which he interacts with each and every person in his life. His message as coach, more accurately teacher, is that success comes from commitment, sacrifice, and love."

Sports Faith International named Frank Allocco its 2012 Coach of the Year. Frank Allocco is an extraordinary example of an outstanding role model in the world of sports: successful in the win-loss column, and vigilant in the athletic and personal development of players entrusted to his care.

JIM RYUN

"Do you not know that in a race all the runners compete, but only one receives the prize? So run that you may obtain it. Every athlete exercises self-control in all things. They do it to receive a perishable wreath, but we an imperishable. Well, I do not run aimlessly, I do not box as one beating the air; but I pommel my

body and subdue it, lest after preaching to others I myself should be disqualified."

— *1 Corinthians 9:24-27*

As a young student, Jim Ryun wanted to make a team—to be part of something, but he found it difficult. In junior high, he could not make the basketball team. He was even cut from his church's baseball team. He often expressed his feelings to God:

"Dear God, if you've got a plan for my life, I'd appreciate it if you'd show up sooner or later, because it's not really going very well."[53]

Pray and Repeat

After praying over and over again, Ryun's prayers were answered. He began competing in track. At Wichita High School East, Ryun ran track and before long he was setting ambitious goals with his coach, Bob Timmons. He took second place in the mile in his first race and he won every race in high school after that! As a junior in 1964, Ryun was the first high school athlete to break the four-minute mile and his 3:55.3 high school mile record set as a senior, held for about 36 years. Ryun's high school running career was impressive. According to ESPN, five of the six fastest schoolboy miles have been run by Ryun. ESPN named Ryun the best high school athlete ever.[54]

Ryun set the adult mile record twice and his 3:51.1 mark in 1967 stood for about 8 years. In the same year, he set the adult world record for the 1,500 meters at 3:33:1, which stood for over 6 years. Ryun would be remembered as one of the best runners of his day. Although he competed in the 1964, 1968 and 1972 Olympics, he did not have his best performances on the world stage.

Ryun was just a young schoolboy in the 1964 Olympics and he did not medal. The 1968 Olympics took place in high altitude in Mexico City and many track athletes were adversely affected. Ryun was the favorite of the 1,500-meters, but Kip Keino from Kenya easily took the gold, while Ryun won the silver. Ryun would often run in the back of the pack and move up quickly towards the end of the race. Keino and a fellow Kenyan pushed the pace of the race and Ryun simply could not catch up in time in the high altitude.

In the 1972 Olympics, the stage was set for another showdown between Ryun and Keino, but Ryun was tripped and disqualified. After the race, Ryun met his wife in the stadium corridor and prayed. His prayer was simple: "God I need Your help." He had no idea what might be the next step in his life. His appeal was rejected. It took time for Ryun to get past the injustice he felt and for him to forgive those involved. He decided in the end that everyone must forgive. That God has a plan for each one of our lives. That he had a responsibility to reflect the "likeness of Christ."

At home, Ryun had better luck and he won the AAU mile for three straight years, 1966-1968.

In 1996, he was involved in carrying the Olympic torch across Kansas. He was encouraged by Congressman Todd

Tiahrt to run for Congress. He won the election and served 10 years as a Representative from Kansas, from 1996-2007.

Jim Ryun has conducted a running camp for many years that mostly serves high school students. His camp offers instruction geared toward developing the total runner – physically, mentally and spiritually. Campers learn how to apply racing and training strategies. They hear from top Christian athletes who will share how their faith has helped them reach their fullest potential.

RON MEYER

Finally, be strong in the Lord and in the strength of his might.

— Ephesians 6:10,

In life, we fight the good fight, run the good race. But often it takes time before we understand where we are going and the best way to get there. For Christians, life is a journey to faith fulfilled.

Ron Meyer grew up Catholic, but neither he nor his family were particularly engaged in their faith. In fact, Meyer remembers himself as apathetic. He was much more concerned about athletic performance. Meyer played some college baseball and semi-pro ball out east before deciding at age 20 to quit college and head south.

He went to a casting call in Hollywood, Florida, a city that has a motion picture industry presence like its namesake. He was called back for a shoot. Days before his acting debut, his right eye started to droop. He returned to the east for tests where he was diagnosed with Myasthenia Gravis, one of many muscular dystrophy diseases. The condition worsened and ordinary activities became challenging. Depression followed.

RON MEYER

One Sunday, Meyer attended Mass. At the elevation of the Sacred Host, Meyer profoundly felt the presence of God and his eyes gained full strength. The weakness returned, but then strength was regained at Mass the following week. Meyer recognized that God's hand would guide him through his journey.

The disease never progressed, but Meyer felt its sobering effects. Medicine alleviated most symptoms. He returned to sports and moved to Arizona where his family had settled. He studied scripture, prayed the rosary, joined an active parish. Faith grew. He found God beside him, guiding and loving him.

Meyer decided to follow the will of God. He determined that his role was to communicate to others the truths of his faith. He has not stopped. Meyer is deeply involved in Catholic media. He works for the Eternal Word Television Network (EWTN) that provides around the clock Catholic themed programming. He has created several Catholic video productions including a radio sports program called "Blessed2Play" that he hosts.

Today, Meyer plays racquetball. He is a four time state divisional racquetball champion in Ohio and West Virginia. He lives in Bloomingdale, Ohio, with his wife Julie and their three children Anna, Angelica, and Maria.

IN HIS MIGHTY POWER
When it comes to family, I think
We should take the approach of Abraham
Lincoln after the Civil War. He said,
"...with malice toward none, with charity
toward all." Everyday is a clean slate.
Let us not encourage complaints or
gossip. We will need God's mighty power.
Pope Saint John Paul II said, "To maintain

A joyful family requires much from both
the parents and the children. Each member
of the family has to become, in a
special way, the servant of the other."

Grandpa George believed in daily exercise.
He said, "Never go to bed a loser."
My father believed in daily abstinence.
He wanted no one to be a boozer.
There is no shortage of advice.
Some of it is really quite nice.
My favorite advice is that which is sought.
Regardless, we have to do what we ought.
I have some advice of my own.
I thought I'd write instead of phone.
Win, in His mighty power.
Then, please, go take a shower.

— Patrick McCaskey

TOM BENSON

Tom Benson is a New Orleans native who at only 17 years old enlisted in the Navy in 1945 and served in the Pacific aboard the USS South Dakota. Later, Benson was highly successful in business and built up a chain of automobile dealerships, which led to his ownership of several banks.[55]

In 1985, successful businessman Tom Benson became the owner and Managing General Partner of the New Orleans Saints Football Club. It would be a challenging undertaking to build the team into a contender. The first two decades saw a small margin of success. And just before the team got much better, disaster struck in 2005 when Hurricane Katrina ravaged the Gulf. The Saints could not play their 2005 season games in their home, the Louisiana Superdome, and for a time, the viability of New Orleans as a professional football venue came into question after the economic injury and population decline that resulted.

Benson's Efforts on Behalf of New Orleans

As New Orleans continued to struggle economically in 2009, the New Orleans Saints finished their season 13–3 and went on to win the Super Bowl. It was one of the most memorable seasons in NFL history and certainly a boost to the spirit of the city and the region. On the field, Benson's coach, Sean Payton, and his quarterback, Drew Brees, have helped establish the Saints as consistent contenders over the last several seasons. Saints' fans appreciate the effort.

Off the field, Tom Benson has had a positive impact on the community. In fact, many believe he purchased the Saints to keep them home in the "Crescent City." Those who know him say that the club's charitable involvement has been among his most rewarding endeavors. The Saints' players, coaches, and staff donate their time in volunteer work and charitable outreach. Millions of dollars have been raised by Benson and his team for community causes through the Saints Hurricane Katrina Fund and Gulf Coast Renewal Fund. The New Orleans Saints partners with local youth-oriented charities to reach as many children as possible. Over 45 foundations and agencies receive monetary donations from the Saints each year. Benson has also worked closely with the Ochsner Foundation Hospital in New Orleans with the Establishment of the Tom and Gayle Benson Cancer Center, a $20-million treatment complex.

Among many honors, Benson and the Saints received the Good Samaritan Award in Philanthropy. Benson himself was awarded Loyola University of New Orleans' Integritas Vitae Award, and he has been inducted into the Sports Faith Hall of Fame.

Patrick McCaskey's Three Suggestions

If we have to punt let's consider that a turnover.

Let's get way ahead so we can play everyone. When it's time to make substitutions, let's not sing, "Send in the Clowns."

Don't let the players worry about playing time. When we win the championship, everyone will letter.

Fellowship of Christian Athletes

Fellowship of Christian Athletes "demonstrate steadfast commitment to Jesus Christ and His Word through integrity, serving, teamwork and excellence." We did not have a Fellowship of Christian Athletes group at my high school and I wish we had.

I have seen the movie "Chariots of Fire" many times and I could easily see it again. When I was in high school I felt like Harold Abrahams from the movie who said, "They'll lead you to the water, but they won't let you drink." Abrahams was constantly humiliated by the anti-Semitism of his day. I felt like Abrahams who raced to get back at the world, to take his tormenters on "one by one and run them off their feet."

After college, I became associated with the Fellowship of Christian Athletes. I attended summer conferences. The experiences there reminded me of some lines from the Hebrew poet Yehuda Amichai. "The passing years have calmed me, and brought healing to my heart, and rest to my eyes."

At the FCA summer conferences that I attended, athletes played with exemplary, gentlemanly sportsmanship and actually prayed for the referees. Everyone had a great deal of good, clean fun. It was very much like the competition in "Chariots of Fire."

Also in "Chariots of Fire" was Eric Liddell, a "muscular Christian." His missionary father told him, "You can praise the Lord by peeling a spud if you peel it to perfection. Run in the Lord's name and let the world stand back in wonder."

Now my motivation is similar to Eric Liddell's. He said, "God made me for a purpose, but He also made me fast. When I run I feel His pleasure. To give that up would be to hold him in contempt." Abrahams described Liddell: "I've never seen such desire, commitment in a runner. He runs like a wild animal. It unnerves me."

The Biblical principles on which Eric Liddell based his life can be learned at the FCA summer conferences. His widow said, "He always spent the first hour of the day in Bible reading, prayer, and planning the day's concerns. He was never shocked or judgmental about other people's conduct or problems. He could be very naughty himself and he had a remarkable sense of humor. His greatest gift was his understanding of people. They felt it and came to him constantly for help."

If it had not been for the Christian leadership of Bruce Bickel, I might still be a bachelor. I am very grateful to Bruce. In the words of Paul McCartney, "No more lonely nights." Bickel was the original Chicago area director of the Fellowship of Christian Athletes. He and his wife, Anita, conducted the Bear Bible studies. I began attending in 1977. Bruce and Anita hosted the Bear Bible study campout in a Wheaton forest preserve. Assistant coach Ross Fichtner and his wife, Karen, defensive lineman Gary Hrivnak and his wife Linda, safety Doug Plank and his wife, Nancy, and I attended. For respectful comic relief, I arrived, after the camp had been pitched, in a suit and a tie with American Tourister luggage. I had the assignment of bringing the toilet paper, which I did.

Bruce had told me that he would bring a sleeping bag for me. He forgot. So I slept in the same sleeping bag with Bruce and Anita. Bruce insisted on sleeping in the middle. I did not sleep well that night. I fell asleep during Bruce's financial seminar the next day.

On Saturday, October 15, 1977, there was a farewell dinner for Bruce and Anita in the main dining hall of Wheaton College. Bruce left Chicago to join the national FCA staff in Kansas City. Chicago FCA Chairman Dale Bonga said, "It is very difficult to lose Bruce and Anita, but we decided to share them with the nation."

I met Wayne Gordon, the pastor of the Lawndale Community Church, that night. I did not get to know him well until the Michigan FCA summer conference in 1979. I attended Gordy's dating seminar.

He told me about Genesis 2:21, "So the Lord God caused the man to fall into a deep sleep."

Gordy explained that God was preparing Adam for marriage while he slept. When he awoke, he was ready for a partner.

God does not give a partner to a man until he is ready for her. In the meantime, we are not to be on the prowl. We are to sleep while God is preparing us. I believed that these things were true because Gordy had heard them from Bruce Bickel.

I had the privilege of attending the FCA Leadership Workshop with Bruce Bickel as the main speaker on Saturday, February 23, 1985. I learned that God is looking for leaders who have responsive hearts, who deal honestly and truthfully, who are willing to stand alone, and who understand that God makes the difference.

As a leader, if you are going to meet people's needs, you have to stop for them. You have to ask their needs. You have to trust in God for the results.

My favorite Biblical example of leadership is Jesus. He washed the feet of His Apostles. He was called to serve, not be served.

Here's a passage that reminds me of my wife:

Love is Unselfish

A good wife who can find?
  She is far more precious than jewels.
The heart of her husband trusts in her,
  and he will have no lack of gain.
She does him good, and not harm,
  all the days of her life.
She seeks wool and flax,
  and works with willing hands.
She is like the ships of the merchant,
  she brings her food from afar.
She rises while it is yet night
  and provides food for her household
  and tasks for her maidens.
She considers a field and buys it;
  with the fruit of her hands she plants a vineyard.
She girds her loins with strength
  and makes her arms strong.
She perceives that her merchandise is profitable.
  Her lamp does not go out at night.

She puts her hands to the distaff,
  and her hands hold the spindle.
She opens her hand to the poor,
  and reaches out her hands to the needy.
She is not afraid of snow for her household,
  for all her household are clothed in scarlet.
She makes herself coverings;
  her clothing is fine linen and purple.
Her husband is known in the gates,
  when he sits among the elders of the land.
She makes linen garments and sells them;
  she delivers girdles to the merchant.
Strength and dignity are her clothing,
  and she laughs at the time to come.
She opens her mouth with wisdom,
  and the teaching of kindness is on her tongue.
She looks well to the ways of her household,
  and does not eat the bread of idleness.
Her children rise up and call her blessed;
  her husband also, and he praises her:
"Many women have done excellently,
  but you surpass them all."
Charm is deceitful, and beauty is vain,
  but a woman who fears the Lord is to be praised.
Give her of the fruit of her hands,
  and let her works praise her in the gates.

— Proverbs 31:10-31

Thank You Note

Thank you for saying I do
Thank you for our children too.

Proverbs 31 describes the ideal wife.
It also describes our wonderful life.

Even when you are on the phone,
I never really feel alone.

Our loving marriage is in its thirty-second orbit.
I do not regret that I have never met
Russian Olympic gymnast Olga Korbut.
You have given up the cello
For crocheting, fencing for cross-
Stitching, tennis for sewing, and
Clinical nurse specializing for
your Community Bible Study.

Like the Quaker woman in the John
Wayne movie, "Angel and the Badman,"
You help me with Bible quotes.
You respect my allergy to goats.

In a bucket, we carry a tune
Because we are on our honeymoon

— Patrick McCaskey

Where Would I Be?

Dan Duddy with Donovan Catholic High School Player

I have not come to call the righteous but sinners to repentance.

— Luke 5:32

Being part of professional football for 40 years provides a solid perspective on both success and failure. You see athletes achieve great things while very young, especially those who gather around them good solid people. They struggle like everyone else, but they chart a course of faith and family that leads to peace.

Unfortunately, you see other athletes who are unprepared for the money or the stress. Sometimes they connect with people who are not good for them. Some seem to just self-destruct amidst the fame and fortune.

But, many of those who struggle, survive, and then thrive. They look at their lives and ask themselves where would they be without faith—without Christ. Often a good parent or coach can help.

DAN DUDDY'S VIRTUOUS PROGRAM

Dan Duddy is the football coach at Donovan Catholic High School in Toms River, New Jersey. The school has many outstanding programs which all lead the following aspirations for students: Faith is the foundation that helps lead students towards these objectives—a faith that is developed and grows strong through the school's faith-based education and sports. Coach Duddy begins his efforts before the school year begins.

> Become Who You Want.
> Believe in Yourself.
> Change the World.
> Create the Future.
> Exceed Your Potential.
> Experience a College Environment.
> Express Your Creativity.
> Know That You Matter.

The football staff and team attend a week long "Virtue Camp" every year before their first game. They live in rustic cabins and have "Virtue sessions" and grueling workouts. Everything they do at camp involves the whole team and the whole staff.

The team learns to pray the rosary and Mass is offered. Duddy and staff have Bible study. Players fill out their "life goal sheets" and are assigned a mentor. The players write home to Mom.

Duddy talks about pro-life, responsibility, sex and respect for women, marriage, and temptation. When someone hollers "We Are?" the team responds in unison "The Sons of Thunder!" The reference is to James and John, the sons of Zebedee, the tough, feisty, and bold apostles. Much is accomplished at camp and players bring their best to the playing field when the season starts.

The team has spiritual Bible sessions every night before game day. Film clips, Bible verses, and discussion follow a "theme of the week." Athletes reflect and record in writing the effects of "Our Virtue Program" at season's end. They have team Masses before every home game in the morning. The program has had a big impact on the athletes and the Donovan Catholic community.

A coach becomes part of the community and impacts players long after graduation. Duddy and his wife Maura have eight children. Their lives among the tightly knit community came closer together when the Duddy's son Francis died in a car accident in 2014. Any doubts about what the community shared with the Duddy's and the hold that faith has on the Donovan community was clear in the aftermath of tragedy.[56] Thousands and thousands of people came to Francis's wake. A miraculous expression of the community's love followed. Dan Duddy said:[57]

"We would rather those things have been revealed in a different way, but once we opened up our hearts to letting it truly become revealed to us and take it in, the death of Francis—which was unbelievably tragic—became triumphant. We became so, so, so profoundly secure in the world of the people that are around us…"

"I let loose and did my anger thing with our Lord. 'Why the heck am I getting on my knees, literally every night, praying please protect my family and praying the prayer that you taught us?' Thy will be done. Protect them, bring them home and thy will be done. And then the two of them came together. The Lord brought my son home. Thy will was done. My son is home, and that's when I found out my son was more a child of God in heaven than he was of my own, and then I was put in my place. It was a spiritual revelation."

Before Donovan's first game, it holds a Father-Son Jersey Night, a pasta dinner in which fathers and other male role models attend. Fathers of the senior players talk about their sons to the crowd. According to Duddy, "They speak about things that have happened in the young man's life that really impressed them, and then in front of 200 people or so he flat out says, 'I love you son,' and hands the jersey off to him."

Duddy recalled having this moment with Francis when he played for him in 2012 and he said:

"Francis is often a misunderstood guy. But Francis will never ever misunderstand you because Francis knows the hearts of everyone that is around him."

And Duddy carries on to help shape young men who will go on to become great leaders, husbands and fathers. Duddy is a recipient of the Sports Faith Virtues of Saint Paul Award. Those virtues are discipline, concentration, respect for school rules, excellence in effort of competition, leadership, confidence, fair play, teamwork, sacrifice, determination, resilience, and respect for others.

Rich Garza's Ministry to Youth

In his school days, Rich Garza played for the Hurricanes of Liberty High School in Bethlehem, Pennsylvania, where he earned 10 varsity letters while participating in football, basketball, baseball, and track and field. He went on to Temple University and he played football for the Owls. He became an offensive lineman for the Philadelphia Eagles and the Denver Broncos of the NFL as well as the Philadelphia Stars and San Antonio Gunslingers of the USFL. At 6-foot-1 and 270 pounds, Garza opened up some big holes for his offense.

Garza battled alcohol abuse as a young man, even while excelling on the football field. He sought a deeper relationship with Jesus as he struggled to turn his life around. One day in team chapel service while in Tampa Bay for a football game, he heard NFL chaplain Dr. Ira Lee Eshelman speak. Garza surrendered his life to Jesus Christ. He was inspired to minister to young people and educate parents on the hidden toll of alcohol abuse. He is a tireless evangelist who has spoken to over a million young people in schools and other settings.

He tells his audience to make sure they have the right friends. Kids "make bad choices when they listen to bad voices"–"bad company corrupts good morals." Garza advocates eliminating things in our lives that are slowing us down from following our faith. He says "fix our eyes on Jesus and his word."

Garza understands troubled kids and he speaks very clearly to his audiences. He says "Freedom is not about doing what you want to do; freedom is doing what you ought to do." He reminds kids that "If you're breaking the law, you're not going to have your freedom." He backs up his talks with statistics on young people who end up in prison. He drives home the likely impact of bad choices on young people. He strongly states:

"When God speaks to you, obey immediately."

He tells kids to avoid looking at themselves as losers; he admonishes them to look at themselves as *choosers*. It's the choices they make that will help define their lives. He speaks simply so every kid in his audience can understand his points.

Garza encourages his audience to not just read the Bible, but study it. He says that when we surrender our lives to Jesus, we can come to know peace, we come to understand that He died for our sins. According to Garza,

"...live like a believer and then you are ready when
someone questions what you are doing. Be ready to
give an answer."

Garza is a minister and evangelist who served as a speaker for Dr. Eshelman's Sports World, Inc. ministries. Garza is active in his local church and now works for the Soldiers for Christ Ministry. He is also Co-Chaplain for the San Antonio Spurs professional basketball team. When the big man talks, kids listen and relate to him. They see someone who has struggled himself, but who has a strong direction in his own life. Rich Garza is no longer playing football, but for his new team he is still punching holes in the opposition. Rich Garza and his wife Jan have four children: Kelly, Rich, David, and Danny.

MOVING ON
In relation
To the parable
Of the prodigal son,
I have been the younger son.
I have been rebellious.
I have been the older son.
I have been resentful.
Now my goal is to be the father.
Forgive others as I have been forgiven.

— Patrick McCaskey

SAL BANDO TURNS HIS LIFE OVER TO THE LORD

Sal Bando was born in Cleveland, Ohio, and grew up a tough kid who played several sports. As a high school quarterback, Bando broke his toe early in one game and still scored five touchdowns.[58] He played baseball for Arizona State University and was elected to the College Baseball Hall of Fame in 2013.

Bando played for the Kansas City/Oakland Athletics and was a team leader and major contributor to the franchise's legendary success in the 1970s. He served as team captain, hit for power, and often ranked high in RBIs while collecting many walks. He moved to the Milwaukee Brewers and after his retirement as a player, he served as General Manager. He was a sixteen-year major leaguer, a four-time All-Star, and a three-time World Series Champion. Well respected by his peers, Bando finished second in MVP votes in 1971, third in 1974, and fourth in 1973. He has been a sportscaster, a baseball executive, and a businessman.

It wasn't always easy. Bando recalled going through a terrible slump in the 1975 season. [59] He went from the best hitter on the Oakland Athletics to the worst. Bando went from batting first in the lineup to batting eighth. His slump was so bad that he couldn't hit and he couldn't field either. Thousands watched his slump continue day after day at the ballpark.

Things got worse and worse for Bando. He was short tempered around home—disagreeable at the ball park. His wife Sandra sought solace with a friend, Jackie Dark, the wife of A's manager Alvin Dark. Alvin Dark had been known as a tempestuous manager in his first stint with the A's, but he had undergone a transition in faith that had completely changed him before he began his second stint as Oakland manager. Jackie Dark talked to Sandra about committing to Christ, putting her problems in His hands. She recommended a book to her called *His Stubborn Love* by Joyce Landorf. Sandra read the book and listened to Jackie. She was moved and she put her life in Christ's hands. She turned herself over to Him. She prevailed on her husband to do the same, but he resisted. One day while she was out of town, he picked up the Landorf book and read it while alone in the house. Bando thought of himself as a good Christian, but he saw that he had not gone far enough in his faith, that he had not turned his life over to the Lord. The transition was fast. Bando looked to the Lord and made Him the center of his existence and his life turned around. It was late in the season, his play improved on the field and he changed his ways at home. He became more patient and was tuned into his wife and his sons. His life improved.

Bando did not check his competitiveness. In talking about his faith and life in sports, Bando quipped:

As I grew in my faith, it did not stop me from trying to take a guy out in a double play.[60]

Bando's courage on the field as a player is now followed by his many faith driven activities off-the-field after his career. Bando is a Board Member of Catholic Athletes for Christ (CAC) an organization that serves Catholic athletes in their practice of faith—created in response to Pope Saint John Paul II's call to evangelize the world of sports.[61]

Bando and other Christ-centered athletes encourage Catholic athletes in the practice of their faith. CAC arranges for Masses to be said at stadiums across the country and hosts an annual retreat for baseball players. Also through the organization, a panel of athletes and coaches—both retired and active—speaks about how their Catholic faith is an essential part of their careers. The aim is to evangelize the world of sports by offering up solid Catholic role models.

Bando said the effort is expanding year after year. "It's like having faith in a foxhole. When you go through tough times, and let's face it, in baseball you fail more than you succeed, guys are looking for a little divine inspiration, a little peace in their lives. At least if it is there they have a choice."[62]

The former MLB slugger also led "Batting 1000," a pro-life outreach of professional baseball players. This initiative culled up a great deal of courage on the part of many athletes when involvement risked loss of endorsements and harsh criticism from media sources. Sal Bando was inducted into the Sports Faith Hall of Fame in 2013.

MORE THAN WINNING
What we need,
God provides.
What we want
Is another story,

Not necessarily a Cinderella one.
When in doubt,
Take it to a higher court.
Pray about it.
Don't despair.
Once you stop trying,
Things get worse in a hurry.
Loving is more than winning.
So is forgiving.
Our mandate is
To love God and each other.
In our attempts to love,
We are often funny.
As far as I know,
All my apologies are up-to-date.

— Patrick McCaskey

SAINT AUGUSTINE AND HIS MOTHER SAINT MONICA

Saint Monica is remembered as the mother of Saint Augustine.
Monica was an innocent and pious Catholic who was married
to a Pagan named Patritius, who was likely a drinker as well
as a carouser. Monica had three children: sons Augustine and
Navigius, and a daughter, Perpetua. She wanted her children
to be Baptized and brought up in the faith, but she was hin-

dered by Patritius until he himself was converted. Patritius died after his Baptism and left Monica a widow.

Monica spent many hours praying for her son Augustine's conversion and salvation. Saint Augustine would look back on his youth as a time of reckless immoral behavior.

Augustine was promiscuous, lazy, and a reveler. Augustine took up with a mistress with whom he had a son and lived with for many years. Saint Monica was a devout Christian and impressed those around her by her faith and prayer life. Augustine's mistress was not an acceptable wife and he hated to leave her, but he did. He took his son Adeodatus (gift from God). Further consternation resulted from Augustine's adoption of Manichaeism. Manichaeism was a popular religion at the time that divided the world between good and evil principles with things material considered evil and things immaterial intrinsically good. This dualistic theology was at best a heresy. Monica was so disturbed by this turn in her son, that she originally barred the door to him.

As Monica did all her life, she prayed and prayed and prayed. She was assisted by Saint Ambrose in converting Augustine. Biographical information on Monica is sketchy at best, but it was suggested that she was at least tempted by drink and managed to fight it off. Her ability to avoid the destructive nature of vice as well as her incredible faith and untiring prayer life has made her a patron saint of alcoholics. Saint Monica's practice of prayer has stood out for Christians over the centuries.

Saint Augustine went on to give his wealth to the poor, his life to the priesthood, and his labors to the Catholic community of his time. Bishop Augustine is considered one of the greatest Christian writers and a Doctor of the Church.

Alcoholism is a disease that is passed down over the generations. Three generations of my family were alcoholics until my father put it on hold. When he was fifteen, he had five beers while singing in a saloon one night. His head was spinning. He came home and said to his mother, "I'll never drink again." I followed his example and have stayed away from it. I believe I am a better man for it.

Saint Augustine's Prayer to the Holy Spirit

Breathe in me, O Holy Spirit, that my thoughts may all be holy. Act in me, O Holy Spirit, that my work, too, may be holy. Draw my heart, O Holy Spirit, that I love but what is holy. Strengthen me, O Holy Spirit, to defend all that is holy. Guard me, then, O Holy Spirit, that I always may be holy.

— Saint Augustine

GUY CHAMBERLIN AT FORT KEARNEY

Paying It Back

If you can't feed a hundred people, then just feed one.

— *Mother Teresa*

We hear so many stars today talk about "giving back" or "paying it back." The idea is that with all one's personal success and riches, the world needs help. One way or another, we need to reach down inside and help. Interestingly enough, often the payback comes most generously from someone who has not enjoyed the superstar treatment at all.

Berlin Guy "Champ" Chamberlin

Berlin Guy "Champ" Chamberlin[63] was born on January 16, 1894 on a farm outside of Blue Springs, Nebraska, the third child born to Elmer E. Chamberlin and Anna Tobyne Chamberlin. After graduating from Blue Springs High School he attended Nebraska Wesleyan in Lincoln and played football. After his sophomore year, he transferred to the University of Nebraska.

Chamberlin played halfback at Wesleyan, and in 1911, his team won seven games with no losses. Chamberlin made the Omaha World Herald's All-Nebraska team. In his second year at Wesleyan, the football team suffered two losses, but Chamberlin once again gained all-state honors. He was 6-foot-2 and thin, but a strong aggressive running back, who knocked tacklers off their feet. As a defensive end, he broke plays up in the opposition backfield.

Clocked at 10 seconds for the 100-yard dash, Chamberlin threw the discus, and he ran the 100-yard dash, the 440, and the half mile.[64] As a sophomore, Chamberlin lettered in football, track, and baseball.[65] He also found time to teach Sunday school at the First Methodist Church.

As a transfer student at the University of Nebraska, the newcomer was ridiculed. Chamberlin was friendly and sociable, but when he got a chance to show his football prowess in practice as a defensive end, he started knocking out varsity Cornhuskers like shooting ducks. Like many great players, he would exhibit a calm demeanor off the field and become something else entirely inside the white chalk lines. At the University, he played end and halfback in 1914. He scored 9 touchdowns and his team posted a 7–0–1 record winning the Missouri Valley Conference Championship. In his senior year in 1915, on offense, he moved primarily to end. Nebraska finished 8–0; they won the conference championship again. All-American Chamberlin scored 15 touchdowns.

In that 1915 season, Chamberlin and the Huskers had a showdown with a strong Notre Dame team coached by Jesse Harper with Assistant Coach Knute Rockne. Rockne instructed his players on apparent weaknesses in Chamberlin's running game, but Chamberlin displayed none. The game was a tight match, but Nebraska prevailed, 20–19. Chamberlin scored on two end-around plays and he passed for another touchdown.

After serving in the U.S. Army as a Second Lieutenant in World War I from 1918-1919 as a weapons instructor stateside, Chamberlin was recruited by Jim Thorpe to play on the Canton Bulldogs. The Bulldogs were owned by Ralph E. Hay who owned a dealership in town that sold Jordan Hupmobiles and Pierce-Arrows. Hay would be remembered for his work with George Halas and others to establish the NFL itself.

Chamberlin played halfback as well as offensive and defensive end for the Bulldogs. The Bulldogs in 1919 were a semipro team. Most historians look at the year 1920 as the beginning of professional football—at least as a formerly organized activity.

A young engineer in charge of the Staley athletic teams, George Halas, scouted Chamberlin and asked him to join his industrial—soon to become professional—team. Chamberlin played with Halas and the Staleys from 1920-1921. The 1920 team was located in Decatur and was called the Decatur Staleys because it was owned by the Staley Starch Company. In addition to football, Chamberlin also played on the Staleys' baseball team that featured the great Iron Man Joe McGinnity as player-manager.

Guy Chamberlin played left end and Halas played right end. The Staleys also featured Hall of Famer George Trafton, Jimmy Conzelman, Halas's future Bears' partner Dutch Sternaman, and others. The media lauded the excellent wing play of the Staleys—that of Halas and Chamberlin. The Staleys final game at the end of the season against the Akron Pros was billed as the league championship.[66] The Akron Pros and the Decatur Staleys fought to a 0–0 tie. The Pros took the championship based on their record.

When the economy was hit by a recession, Mr. Staley turned team ownership over to Halas for 1921 with some seed money. The team was called the Chicago Staleys in 1921 and became the Chicago Bears in 1922.

In 1921, the Chicago Staleys captured the championship with a 9–1–1 record. Chamberlin played in every game. After the season, he joined his former team, the Canton Bulldogs, as player-coach for the 1922 season. He scored seven touchdowns in 1922 and his 42 points made him leading scorer for the team. Canton's 10–0–2 record gave Chamberlin's team the league championship. Owner Ralph Hay sold the Bulldogs before the 1923 season, but took time to praise those involved:

> *The assistance of my organization, the loyal support of the Canton fans and the wonderful harmony that Coach Chamberlin brought into the heart of every player who was with this team in 1922 was the fundamental reason for our success.*[67]

With a record of 11–0–1 in 1923, the Bulldogs wrapped up another championship. An amalgamation of players from two teams formed the Cleveland Bulldogs that Chamberlin led to a 7–1–1 season in 1924 and another league championship.

After the 1924 season, Chamberlin moved on to play and coach the Frankford Yellow Jackets for the 1925 and 1926 seasons. Frankford itself is a neighborhood in northeast Philadelphia. Chamberlin settled into the area, rented a home, pitched for the American Legion in the baseball season, and worked as a truck driver in the off season. Guy Chamberlin brought it all together for the Yellow Jackets in 1926 when they ended the season at 14–1–2 for Chamberlin's fourth NFL Championship.

After an abbreviated season with the Cardinals in 1927, Chamberlin's playing days were over and he did not believe professional football had a future, so he left the game. Football fans look back at Chamberlin's record and wonder how anyone could win four championships coaching three different teams in 5 years. But for many, Chamberlin's accomplishments have been lost in the midst of time.

After Football

Guy followed in his father's footsteps after his football career and farmed. For the most part, there was very little hero worship going around upon his return to Gage County. Depression, draught, and dust must have dampened enthusiasm for what Guy Chamberlin had done. Unlike modern players, there would have been no expectations that his college or professional football career was going to make his fortune. Like so many athletes of his day, he struggled to adjust to a life after his professional career. He and his brothers would live around the farm and at times each of them would be called to run it. As older farm couples are prone to do, Guy

Chamberlin's parents, Elmer and Anna, moved into town, but Elmer kept his hands in the operation. Elmer lived to be 96 years old. Eventually, the Chamberlin farm would be sold in the 1950s.

After his years in sports, life was not easy for Guy Chamberlin although certainly he had been one of the most gifted athletes of his time. In middle age, Chamberlin would have bouts with various health issues that would separate him from farming and some other physically difficult jobs. He would later serve in a state prison reformatory as a state agricultural agent. It would be working with troubled young men at the reformatory that Chamberlin would hit his stride again. Helping underdogs do their best was a natural fit for Chamberlin. In some way, this was Chamberlin's pay back. To console and motivate those who had committed crimes while young men—boys who were broken. One of the greatest coaches in NFL history was back coaching again.

Guy Chamberlin passed away in Lincoln, Nebraska, on April 4, 1967 at the age of 73.

The University of Nebraska created the Guy Chamberlin Trophy in 1967—presented to the senior player who exemplifies the qualities of Guy Chamberlin. Chamberlin found his place preserved in the College Football Hall of Fame in 1962 and the Pro Football Hall of Fame in 1965. At Chamberlin's enshrinement, Canton teammate Doc Elliott called Chamberlin simply "the winningest guy of all time."[68]

George Halas, who had seen it all from the beginning of professional football into the modern era, wrote:

He had all the attributes of a great football player and
as you can imagine in those early days players were
far more rugged than they are today...professional
football was very fortunate in having a man of his
caliber as one of its pioneers.[69]

HIGH SCHOOL RIVALS SHOW OF
FAITH AND CHARITY

When John Weiger was a freshman football player for Montini
Catholic Illinois, he developed a rare form of leukemia that
carried into his sophomore season. The team visited their sick
teammate at the University of Chicago Hospital to cheer him
up. They prayed for him.

The Weiger family incurred substantial debt from the cost of
John's treatment. Montini athletic director Bob Landi reached
out to his Aurora Christian counterpart, Dan Beebe, before the
teams' scheduled football game on October 12, 2012. A zeal-
ous fundraising effort would follow for the family, while John
battled for his life.

When the Montini Catholic Broncos played the Aurora
Christian Eagles in Lombard on October 12, both teams met at
the 50 yard line and prayed together. Both teams were defend-
ing state champs within their respective state divisions. The
game went back and forth to the very end with Montini taking
the lead in the final few minutes to win, 31–27.

On November 4, 2012, John Weiger died. Responding
to Weiger's struggles brought two teams and school commu-

nities closer. The Aurora Christian team attended John's funeral. At the state championships at the University of Illinois, the Montini Catholic team showed up in the stands of the 3A title game wearing white shirts in support of Aurora Christian. The Aurora Christian team showed up in the stands of the 5A title wearing orange shirts in support of Montini Catholic.

Both schools demonstrated Christian values and character. Montini Catholic and Aurora Christian are great examples of winning championships with sportsmanship. The schools were honored by Sports Faith International as the High School Teams of the Year 2012.

DARRELL MILLER PLAYING BALL FOR YOUTH

Darrell Miller was a professional baseball player who played five seasons for the California Angels from 1984-88. He played 97 career games behind the plate, 95 in the outfield, 16 at first base, eight as a designated hitter, and one at third base. Miller played three seasons at California State Polytechnic University, Pomona. He is a member of one of the most successful sports families in history. His brother, former Indiana Pacers guard Reggie Miller, was a standout player in the NBA and his sister Cheryl Miller was a part of the 1984 United States Olympic gold medal-winning women's basketball team. She is regarded as one of the greatest players of all-time.

Today, Miller serves as the director of Major League Baseball's first Urban Youth Academy, owned and operated by Major League Baseball. The academy is located on the campus of Compton (California) Community College where it provides free instruction in both baseball and softball to Southern California youth between the ages of 8-17. It is establishing itself as a training ground for future baseball and softball players and those who may seek a career in other areas that support the game. The academy's mission is to break down barriers facing youth interested in baseball and sports-related professions and provide them, at no cost, with support and expert instruction in their areas of interest.

Miller is a convert to the Catholic faith and has been a featured speaker at Catholic conferences and adult retreats. Miller was also invited to the Vatican to participate in the first-ever Council on Church and Sports. He has been married to his wife Kelly for 18 years and they have three children: Darrell Jr., Nicole, and Cameron. Kelly and Darrell also led a very successful young adult ministry for 14 years at St. Angela Merici in Brea, California. Miller was inducted into Sports Faith International Hall of Fame in 2012.

DISCIPLINED TO WIN

It's a strain to win
With a double chin.
Twinkie and a Ho-ho
Are not the way to go.
It's not much fun
To run and run,
Unless you're a Finn

Like Lasse Viren.
He won four Olympic golds.
Maybe now he drives and Olds.
(It's not a sin
To be a Finn.)
As track meets draw near,
The choice is quite clear.
Give up all sweets;
Relinquish treats.
Or give up running
For sumo wrestling.

— Patrick McCaskey

My Strength and Shield

The Lord is my strength and my shield;
in him my heart trusts;
so I am helped, and my heart exults,
and with my song I give thanks to him.

— Psalms 28:7

Sometimes things go wrong and then our lives take a turn we never expected. We had ambitions of becoming something great and inspiring and we ended up doing something else completely different. Sometimes the change is disappointing, but often it results in something that makes us better. When we look back at such times, we come to understand that our disappointments were for the best. The Lord was directing us in another direction.

Terry Brennan

Terry Brennan was born in Milwaukee, Wisconsin. Brennan went to grade school in Whitefish Bay, a suburb of Milwaukee. At his home, he practiced the pole vault, the shot put, and the hurdles. He was on the football, hockey, and track teams for Marquette High School in Wisconsin.

When Brennan was a student at the University of Notre Dame, he was president of his sophomore class. He played football under Frank Leahy at Notre Dame graduating in 1949. He played halfback and led the Fighting Irish in receiving and scoring in 1946 and 1947. In 1947, he had a 97-yard kickoff return for a touchdown against Army. He started thirty games and he played on three undefeated teams. He was a philosophy major and he had an 85 average. He was an outstanding student at Notre Dame.

Brennan went on to earn his law degree from DePaul University College of Law while he taught and coached at Mount Carmel High School in Chicago. Brennan's Caravan team won three straight city championships. He went to Mass each day. Mount Carmel remembers Brennan fondly as one if its greatest coaches.

Brennan returned to Notre Dame in 1953 to coach the freshman squad under Leahy and then succeeded Leahy as head coach in 1954. After he had been appointed the head football coach at the University of Notre Dame, a reporter pointed out to him that he was only twenty-five years old. Terry replied, "That's all right. I'll be twenty-six pretty soon." He was a "boy-wonder." In 1955, Rawlings was advertising Terry Brennan footballs, helmets, and shoulder pads in *Boys Life*.

The Irish tallied records of 9–1 and 8–2 in Brennan's first two seasons. His five year record at Notre Dame was 32–18. It wasn't good enough for the school who had been led by Rockne and Leahy even though much was being done at the time to focus on academics. In 1959, Brennan moved on to become the player conditioning coach for the Cincinnati Reds in spring training and eventually he joined a Chicago investment banking firm.

In some ways Brennan's life went from the exceptional to the normal. He became a regular family man and dad. He accomplished remarkable achievements in sports by the time he was 30 years old and then moved on to accomplish great things in his own family. He fought the good fight, finished the race, and kept the faith. Brennan is a member of the Chicagoland Sports Hall of Fame, the Wisconsin Athletic Hall of Fame, and the Sports Faith International Hall of Fame.

BUMPS IN THE ROAD

When I was a junior at Notre Dame High School in Niles, Illinois, I failed the football physical because of a hernia. When I was a senior, I was quarterback on defense and offense. We were 9–0 and outscored our opponents 341–80. There were no playoffs then.

University of Notre Dame assistant coach, Joe Yonto, advised me to go to Cheshire Academy to get another year of playing experience. If I played well at Cheshire, then Notre Dame would seriously consider me for a scholarship.

Coach Yonto wrote a letter about me to Steve Kuk, the Cheshire varsity football coach. Based on that letter, Coach Kuk designed a pro-style offense with me passing often. To prepare for the 1967 Cheshire football season, I ran the mile in 4:37.9—the day after the prom.

Right before I left for Cheshire, my eye doctor, George Jessen, told me that I could not play contact sports. I felt like Marlon Brando in the movie, "On the Waterfront," when he said, "I coulda been a contender."

But when I arrived at Cheshire, an incident occurred that got me out of that mindset. I was standing in line at the bookstore one day before classes began. One student said to another student, "We were going to have a great football team, but the quarterback had to give up football."

The other student asked, "What's his name?"

The first student replied, "Jeb Swift; he hurt his knee."

Then I saw a notice on a bulletin board about going out for cross country. So I did.

One meet was against Choate and Stony Brook at Choate. I surprised the leader, Alan Swanson of Stony Brook, as I came from the back of the pack in the rain and passed him. Then he tried to pass me twice. We ended up tied for first at the finish line. At the social, after the race, I found out that he had played quarterback, but he had to give up playing football because of a knee injury from snow skiing.

I placed 14th in the New England championship race and won a medal. I won the conference championship race on the track around the football field at halftime of the homecoming game. I had 13 races and I won nine, while setting seven course records. My nickname was Roadrunner.

Everyone has hopes and dreams.

Our personal aspirations take a backseat to the will of God. I support my sons' aspirations, but more than anything else, I want my sons to follow Jesus. I want them to know that regardless of what happens in their careers, they are in good hands.

As many parents are asked to do, I was asked to write a letter to my eldest son that he could read on his senior retreat. I was asked again when my second son attended. And finally, I was asked a third time when my youngest son was on retreat. I thought my first letter was so good, that I used it three times.

Dear Son,

When I was a high school freshman, I was calling out the signals as quarterback and my voice cracked. I said, "Ready" (in a deep voice) "Set" (in a high voice). When I was a sophomore, I started two games at end, five games at halfback, and two games at fullback. Then I didn't have to call signals. When I was a junior, I failed the football physical because of a hernia. My voice cracked that day. When I was a senior, I was quarterback on defense and offense; my voice did not crack.

Now you are a high school senior and you are on your senior retreat. You are a very good student. You are on your way to a faith-based college where you can get an excellent education.

Most importantly, let's hope you're on your way to heaven. Regardless of where you go to college, let's keep the ultimate goal in mind. We're interested in schools that emphasize faith, education, and sports. We want to win championships with sportsmanship and we want to get to heaven. I'll be with you at the family retreat Mass.

It's important to grow physically, socially, culturally, and spiritually.

Physically, you are a very good athlete.

Socially, you are a very good family member and a very good friend.

Culturally, you are doing very well in school.

Spiritually, you go to Church and you exhibit sportsmanship. I want you to continue to be a servant leader like Jesus Who washed the feet of His disciples. You are one of my three beloved sons in whom I am well pleased.

Jesus is my role model and I hope and trust that He is yours. Regardless of what others do, we need to do what is right.

We have God's grace and mercy that provide strength. Church and Bible Study and daily devotions keep us on the right path.

Your mother and I are praying that you will continue to grow in the Lord. If you are not called to the priesthood, I hope that you will marry a follower of Jesus, someone like your mother.

I enjoy being with you. You are very good company.

Pride is a sin. So I don't say that I am proud of you. I am grateful that you are my son. Thank you. I love you. It's great to be with you.

Your earthly father,

JEREMY LIN PUTS HIS CAREER IN GOD'S HANDS

Jeremy Lin is an interesting man and NBA player. His parents came from Taiwan to settle here in the United States where Jeremy and his two brothers were born. His dad loves the game of basketball; it rubbed off on his kids. Mom supported anything the kids did that was positive as long as they kept up on their grades. Jeremy is a devout Christian and he thanks God for the good things in his life. He does his best to cast off doubts and discouragement by falling back on his faith.

The Lins settled in Palo Alto and Jeremy became a basketball star in high school. In his senior season, 2005–2006, Palo Alto soared to a 32–1 record and beat a powerful Mater Dei High School, 51–47, to win state in their division. Although considered by many to be one of the best players in California, Lin did not get much scholarship attention going into college. High academics, intelligence, and a superior work ethic made an impression on Harvard and he went out east without a scholarship.

Lin was an excellent college basketball player and his height settled in at 6-foot-3. The All Ivy League guard became one of the best all-around college players. In fact, he was the first player in the history of the Ivy League to record 1,450 points (1,483), 450 rebounds (487), 400 assists (406) and 200 steals (225).

Lin has great respect for his Taiwanese parents and their ancestors who go back to various parts of China, but he is very much an American. Lin does not look like an NBA guard except when he is on the court. And many people have misjudged his abilities based on his ethnicity. He has had a rocky career and his play never seems to be appreciated any place for long.

Un-drafted, Lin has struggled in the pro game since he was originally signed by the Golden State Warriors in 2010.

Playing in San Francisco with its large Asian-American population was marketing heaven for the organization and NBA hell
for Lin. Every time Linn got into a game, the home crowd
would often erupt in applause, but it was a pressure cooker of a
place to play. Lin was not suitably prepared for NBA competition. He was back and forth between the Warriors and their
"D" League team, the Reno Big Horns. In the off-season, he
improved his strength and skills that needed work. Lin had always been relentless at practice and preparation. Yet, Golden
State released him before his second season although he was
much better prepared. Lin was circling at a certain contract
level in the NBA that is vulnerable. Players at a certain depth
on the squad can be signed and released very quickly.

The Houston Rockets picked up Lin in December 2011 and
released him a few weeks later. The New York Knicks picked
him up, but were in no hurry to use him and it looked like he
might get cut again. Injuries and a horrid clutch of losing games
helped get Lin some playing time in February 2012. Lin played
like a super star and his blistering point production helped the
Knicks crack-off 7 wins in a row. He continued to run red hot,
although he struggled with turnovers. The term "Linsanity' was
coined for Lin's fantastic play and later a Linsanity documentary
with that title would be produced that covered his story. Words
cannot describe the incredible shots that Lin was able to make
in all kinds of odd angles and positions for the Knicks. In so
many cases, he would be driving towards the basket, fouled and
falling, but would somehow be able to toss the ball up at an odd
angle and see it drop through the hoop. He also dazzled the

crowd with great passes and a determined super high energy play on every inch of the court. Lin also hit key "three pointers" and game-winners for the Knicks during his "Linsanity" period.

In March, Lin injured his knee and surgery put an end to his season. In a New York minute, fans were treated to a phenomenal performance, but at the season's end, Lin was a restricted free agent.

The Houston Rockets made an excellent bid for Lin's services that the Knicks failed to match. Lin played hot and cold for the Rockets, suffered some injuries, and was traded to the Lakers in July 2014. Many believe he has both the physical gifts and the work ethic to play very well for the right team. Most believe that he has to settle down and play more composed.

Will the Lakers give him the opportunity he needs? He needs to reduce his turnovers and improve his foul shooting. But, he also needs to feel secure for an extended time and he needs a long-term home base—things not necessarily readily available to NBA players. Analysts suggest that Lin has been trying to recreate his magic NY moments, but that bar is a little too high. They believe that he has repeatedly put too much pressure on himself and when he does, it actually hurts his play. Many players suggest though that when Lin's confidence is up, he is hard to stop.

When asked recently about what Laker fans can expect from him, he said:

> *"I am going to be playing for God, and I am going to play the way I've been taught to play and that's going to an up-tempo aggressive style of play."*

Bonnie "the Blur" Blair

On March 18, 1964, Charlie Blair, a Civil Engineer with a passion for skating, packed up the kids and dropped his wife off at the hospital in Cornwall, New York. He drove on to Yonkers with the kids for a skating meet in which he served as timer. His wife was in labor and since she had delivered five kids without a hitch and hospital rules did not allow his presence in the birthing room, he decided to take the kids to the meet.[70] Over the loudspeaker at the event, it was announced that Charlie's wife, Eleanor, had delivered another child. Charlie was pleased.

The Blairs named their child, Bonnie Kathleen Blair. Like other Blair children, she would develop into an amazing athlete. Her athletic accomplishments would combine with her amazing ability to exude joy to those around her.

The Blairs moved to Champaign, Illinois, where Bonnie was raised. She joined the rest of the family in its love for speed skating. When Bonnie was 12 years old, her dad decided she could be an Olympian—Bonnie embraced the goal four years later. When Bonnie was "all in," she dedicated every effort to the sport. Money was tight for the large Catholic family. Her brother Rob and friends established a golf tournament to raise funds for her training. Milwaukee Bucks center and Rob's friend, Jack Sikma, kicked in funds and the Champaign Policemen's Benevolent Association donated enough money for her to train in Milwaukee and travel when necessary for the Sarajevo Olympics in 1984 where she finished eighth in the 500 meter long track race.[71]

Athletes adjust their Olympic training according to where they will be competing. After training in high altitude Butte, Montana, Blair was ready for the Winter Olympics in Calgary in 1988. Before the Olympics, the exuberant athlete appeared on the cover of Life Magazine—a good development for publicity that would help training funding.[72] At about the same time though, she also received news that her father had lung cancer and her brother Rob had inoperable brain cancer. Blair carried on. With her supportive family present along with her faith, she earned gold in the 500 and bronze in the 1,000. Bonnie's biggest supporter, her father, Charlie Blair, died on Christmas, 1989. Her brother Rob would live for many years and fight his disease like an Olympian.

Blair's 1988 Olympic success brought in endorsements that funded her training. Blair had a positive attitude and humility that naturally appealed to fans. Her mother would say that regardless of what success Bonnie had, she would remain the same. In 1992, Blair won gold in the Winter Games in Albertville, France, in both her events—the 500 and 1,000 meter races. The 5-foot-4, 130-pound Blair received the Sullivan Award in 1992 as the United States' top amateur athlete. She kept winning.

In 1994, just two years after the games in Albertville, the Winter Olympics were held in Lillehammer, Norway. The short two-year span was established for this Olympics only so that the winter and summer games could take place in different years going forward. In Lillehammer, Blair once again took gold in both the 500 and 1,000 meter events. She was named "Sportswoman of the Year" by *Sports Illustrated.* Endorsements and awards kept flowing. Her achievements—the first American woman to win five gold medals and the first American Olympian to win gold in the same event in three consecutive Olympics— place her among the greatest female athletes of all time. In 2004, Blair was inducted into the United States Olympic Hall of Fame.

Despite her awards and honors, Blair has always seen herself as a "regular" person with a loving family that showed up in large number at her Olympic contests. Since retiring from skating in 1995, Blair has made a habit of using her gifts both inside and outside the rink. Her notoriety dramatically improved sponsorship to speed skating organizations and she donated funds herself as well. She made a habit of working for others and supporting causes.

Blair married Olympic teammate Dave Cruikshank. Today, the woman who was once called "Bonnie the blur" and her husband Dave have two children, Grant and Blair. Bonnie Blair has coached at the Pettit National Ice Arena in Milwaukee and served on the board of many skating organizations. As a mom, she is careful to manage her outside activities to allow her to focus on rearing her children.

Bonnie has lost several family members to cancer and she has helped raise money for the American Cancer Society. Recently, she has also worked to raise $50,000 to help a water project in Ethiopia called "Wellspring of Hope," run by Catholic Relief Services. Once completed, the initiative will improve the drinking water for 10,000 people.

Bonnie Blair and Greg Brown wrote a children's book called *A Winning Edge* in 1996. When Blair talks to kids she tells them that not everyone can be an Olympian, but she encourages them to find something they love and then dedicate themselves to it. "Be willing to risk your pride and remember to keep a balance in your life, with the help of faith, friends and family. When you do these things you will have a winning edge."[73]

BISHOP PAPROCKI BLOCKS SHOT AGAINST ST. NORBERT COLLEGE

GOOD WORKS AND GOOD HEALTH

BISHOP MALLOY VISITING PRISONERS AND SAYING MASS AT WINNEBAGO COUNTY JAIL AT CHRISTMAS

"This is the beginning of a new day. God has given me this day to use as I will. I can waste it or use it for good, but what I do today is important, because I am exchanging a day of my life for it! When tomorrow comes, this day will be gone forever, leaving in its place something that I have traded for it. I want it to be gain, and not loss; good, and not evil; success, and not failure; in order that I shall not regret the price I have paid for it."

— Anonymous

I

t is important to understand that we do pay a price for everything we do. Our time is valuable and wasting time is well, wasteful. Religious often start the day with prayers and readings. They center themselves for the activities to come and dedicate everything they do to God. Their prayers and readings lead them towards a more healthy relationship with God.

No doubt, if we want a healthy relationship with God, we need to talk—to pray—to read the Bible. For Catholics and several other Christians, there are Sacraments that help provide another means to connect with God.

In addition to keeping our relationship with God healthy, we also need to keep ourselves healthy physically so we are able to work towards the good. This is a challenge for everyone especially our Religious. Catholics know that there is an acute shortage of priests in many different areas. The shortage has given religious leaders a better appreciation for their priests' services and the importance of keeping them in good shape. From small country churches to large cities to remote military posts, sports *and* faith has taken on added importance.

BISHOP DAVID MALLOY PRACTICES FUNDAMENTALS IN ROCKFORD

Bishop David Malloy of the Rockford Diocese in Illinois takes fitness seriously and he wants his Priests in the Diocese to do so as well. He needs healthy priests to run his Diocese and he encourages all those who work for the Diocese to do their best to stay fit. For Malloy personally that means running several times a week at three miles or more an outing and using stairs at the Diocese headquarters rather than the elevator. Just as important as exercise is discipline in his diet. He enters many rooms where abundant food is offered, but frequently grabs a bottle of water and jumps right into conversation. Malloy himself believes that spiritual and physical fitness are connected. "One helps to benefit the other."[74] Malloy's priests all over the Diocese are at various ages and in different conditions of health, but many are now spending time getting exercise and working out.

CARDINAL EDWIN F. O'BRIEN ON THE TREADMILL

Cardinal Edwin F. O'Brien exercises regularly on a treadmill, roots for the Yankees, and leads a spectacularly active life. Like Bishop Malloy, Cardinal O'Brien believes that it is important for priests to take the time to exercise. As a young man he was excellent at handball and baseball. After he was ordained, he moved from Our Lady of Solace in the Bronx to West Point and then on to Vietnam where he was a military chaplain who often moved from one place to another via helicopter. He went to Rome for his Doctoral studies and then worked for Cardinals Cooke and O'Connor back in New York. He served as Archbishop for the Military Service and then moved on to Baltimore where he served as Archbishop there. Pope Benedict XVI elevated O'Brien to cardinal after he had held the title of pro-grand master of the Equestrian Order of the Holy Sepulchre of Jerusalem. This lay order dates back to the 11th century and gives O'Brien duties in the Middle East.[75] O'Brien recently accompanied Pope Francis on his trip to the Holy Land.

Seminarians Starting Early

Fitness is being given more attention at seminaries today. At Mount Angel Seminary, the staff keeps after the seminarians to keep fit and watch their weight. Teams play other schools in the area, seminarians hit the weight room early in the day after prayers, and students are reminded that the body is another gift from God. The importance of fitness for priests is being stressed in many places today and it is much better to establish positive practices early on.

Americans have particularly poor diets. Some studies suggest that priests and other religious are more likely to be overweight than others in our society. Some suggest that well over 40% of American priests are overweight.

Certainly, the scarcity of priests has added pressure to get more things done allowing less time for exercise. As priests in many places live on their own, they are also less likely to create healthy meals for themselves. Bishops and other superiors are so worried about the problem that they are now stressing that regardless of their schedules, priests need to give themselves time for exercising. Better physical health leads to better spiritual health and a healthier mental state.

Father Eric Hoog Joins Navy

Father Eric Hoog felt an early pull towards the Priesthood.

> *"I felt called by God, it's one of those funny things I knew even when I was a small boy, that becoming a priest was something I really wanted to do, so I just simply pursued it."*

Hoog became a Redemptorist Priest at the age of 25 in 1973. After 25 years of being a priest, he wanted to become a Navy chaplain. He gave his reasons in honest straight-forward fashion:

"The reason I became a Navy chaplain was because the Navy was in need of Catholic priests, so I decided to join."

But it was not as easy as signing a document and getting permission from his order. Father Hoog was in poor physical condition. He had to lose over eighty pounds, be able to do over 40 pushups, 60 sit-ups, and run a mile and a half under 13 minutes. He was a long way from meeting these standards.

Luckily he met up with Stew Smith, a Navy SEAL lieutenant and fitness expert who was also looking for something—he was interested in the Catholic Church. Smith guided Father Hoog into a challenging exercise and diet program that methodically moved the motivated Priest forward. At first, it was mostly simple exercise and lots of water. But it became more rigorous over time. With Smith's attention and instruction, Father Hoog lost the weight he needed and became a Navy chaplain. Stew Smith became a Catholic and a fitness guru and author. [76]

Father Hoog served a nine-year tour as a Navy chaplain. He went on three deployments and served in five different locations. He took some time off on sabbatical:

"A sabbatical is essentially a long leave for priests. I decided to take some time off after 33 years or so of being a priest so I could get some studying in, but I tell everybody that I mainly majored in newspapers and espresso."

After several assignments following his sabbatical, Father Hood joined the Marine Corps Air Station at New River North Carolina.[77]

"My primary goal here on New River is service for the immediate community that is aboard the air station, doing the Catholic services, counseling and, of course, confession. My real first immediate goal is to be of service and to become visible to the personnel so that they know they can turn to me."

Father Hoog's ambitious efforts in the priesthood are better served by a man in good physical condition.

Bishop Thomas John Paprocki, the Holy Goalie

The Most Reverend Thomas John Paprocki of the Springfield Illinois Diocese is a church leader who has always been interested in sports and faith. Bishop Paprocki is a hockey goalie and marathon runner. For him exercise is an enjoyable part of his day. He simply says that it "can't be all work and no play." The Bishop believes that Religious like everyone else need exercise and diversion from work.

A hockey fan since childhood on Chicago's south side, Paprocki took up the sport and has continued to play for many years. His teams have won six championships in the Chicago Park District Master Hockey League. Paprocki played goalie for the team called the Lawyers in the over 30 non-checking league.

Bishop Paprocki is affectionately known as the "Holy Goalie" and he has written a book called *Holy Goals for Body and Soul: Eight Steps to Connect Sports with God and Faith.* The Bishop recalls Saint Ignatius's statement "finding God in all things" and suggests that we can find holiness both inside and outside of church. Paprocki suggests that sports and faith can work together to help us experience a greater awareness of God in our lives as we experience "fear, failure, frustration, fortitude, faith, friendship, family, and fun."

Bishop Thomas John Paprocki was inducted into the Sports Faith International Hall of Fame in 2013.

MY PROVERBS

After speaking engagements, desk work brings us back to reality.

Church and Bible Study and daily devotions are very helpful.

Do your best because God doesn't grade on a curve.

Full disclosure of your feelings is highly overrated.

Hatred is self-destructive.

If you can't do one thing, do something else.

If you do nothing but protect yourself, you really stink.

If you drive the speed limit, you don't have to worry about passing anyone.

If you have faith and friendship, tragedy will lead to comedy.

It's important to do charitable work in a charitable manner.

It's wrong to be greedy, even if it's for charity.

Regardless of what others do, we need to do what's right.

Shake it off; get back in the game; do your best.

The Garden of Eden was closed a long time ago.

There is nothing dumber than prejudice.

We're here to live the Gospel.

When you turn the other cheek, don't moon.

Work is a blessing.

Work is work no matter where you find it.

Workouts are recess.

— Patrick McCaskey

Promoting Sports and Virtue

BILL THIERFELDER

"Sport, properly directed, develops character, makes a man courageous, a generous loser, and a gracious victor; it refines the senses, gives intellectual penetration, and steels the will to endurance. It is not merely a physical development then. Sport, rightly understood, is an occupation of the whole man, and while perfecting the body as an instrument of the mind, it also makes the mind itself a more refined instrument for the search and communication of truth and helps man achieve that end to which all others must be subservient, the service and praise of his Creator."[78]

— Pope Pius XII

Bill Thierfelder

Dr. Bill Thierfelder is President of Belmont Abbey College in Belmont, North Carolina, where he and his colleagues challenge students to become truly excellent and virtuous so that in all things God may be glorified. Coming from a modest upbringing in New York City, Dr. Thierfelder is a psychologist who has helped thousands of athletes improve their athletic performances. He received his masters and doctoral degrees in Sports Psychology and Human Movement from Boston University. He was a track and field star and a two-time All-American at the University of Maryland; a National Champion; and a U.S. Olympian. He also served as an NCAA coach. In business, he led York Barbell, Player Management Group, and served as a principal in Joyner Sports Medicine Institute. Thierfelder is the author of a new book called *Less Than a Minute to Go: The Secret to World-Class Performance in Sport, Business and Everyday Life*. His book coaches readers on what it takes to become a world-class performer, how to prepare your mind to win, and how to make peak performance the norm and find passion in daily life.[79]

Thierfelder is a conservative Catholic who frequently speaks to religious audiences. He lives just outside of Charlotte, North Carolina, with his wife, Mary, and their 10 children. He helps put religious people's mind at ease when thinking about sports—especially when they think of sports as a huge influence in the lives of young people. Sports in today's world can carry a lot of negative associations for people. Dr. Thierfelder suggests that we need to "reclaim the game."[80]

In the Halas-McCaskey family, sports and faith have lived together quite well. For our family, the same discipline required for outstanding sports performance is very much like the effort we need to exert to be good Christians. Like the Bishop who asks his Priests to exercise so they can bring a better, healthier self into their ministries, my grandfather promoted athletics as part of our lives so we could become our best and live longer productive and virtuous lives. Similarly, Dr. Thierfelder suggests that athletic effort helps develop the whole person–mind, body and soul. There is a spiritual value in athletics that goes beyond the prayer said before or after practice.[81]

Thierfelder also looks at sports as a thing of beauty with God's handwriting all over it. An athlete whose performance is superb can lead us to reflect on God's handiwork. And for Thierfelder, when play is done for its own sake, "it contemplates the highest things," but if play is selfish, "it is no longer play."

When we practice the old sports adage of giving 100%, we "remain in union with God." There is something special about giving our best. And our athletic efforts should not be outside our spiritual lives. When we secularize our sports, we fall prey of allowing the end to justify the means and that leads to trouble. Having the right frame of mind going into our athletics efforts is key. And as one might expect, Thierfelder's Belmont Abbey College greatly encourages student participation in their athletic programs. The college shares Pope Pius XII quote on sports on its webpage under "Sports and Virtue."

Dr. Bill Thierfelder is a member of the Sports Faith International Hall of Fame.

AUDREY ZAVODSKY'S GOOD RACE

Audrey Zavodsky is a professional race car driver who works for Ford Motor Company in leadership development. She races "clean" and consistently fast. She is the first certified female Hi-Performance driving instructor by the Bondurant School, a Special Vehicle Team Owners Association driving instructor, and a Ford Motor Company proving ground Tier-3 driver. She was also on the first "2 women team" to finish the 13 hour endurance race at Virginia International Raceway. Her racing records include the Global GT Championship, Sports Car Club of America Regional Championship, Panoz GT Pro wins, a Panoz GTS win, several International Motor Sports Association wins, and a class winner at the 24 hours of Morosso.

Zavodsky is a member of the Ford Motor Company Professional Women's Network. She has received numerous awards for her contributions to educational institutions—she was an "academic" long before she became a "racer." Zavodsky received a bachelor of nursing degree and a master's degree in administration from Madonna University—her Ph.D. from Fielding University.

A lover of fast travel, Zavodsky has flown an F-16 fighter jet with the United States Air Force Thunderbirds whom she honors in her presentations. She encourages the students to look at the Air Force for career opportunities as well as pointing out that they are a source of American pride.

Zavodsky developed her racing skills after receiving a doctorate degree. With an academic's appreciation of learning, she attended racing schools to develop her knowledge, skills, and abilities in the sport. Back on the job, Zavodsky also works closely with car focus groups to help bring new ideas and driving experiences into the mix. She evaluates vehicle systems from a performance perspective that translates to best in class characteristics. This is accomplished as she applies her racing and consumer experience to test the various product features. Her ability to communicate helps the engineers to build products that achieve market excellence.

For the racer, lots of hard work in racing, helps prepare you for life. Doing things right is very gratifying. And as she gets older, she has more life experiences to draw on as she continues to work hard and compete.

Zavodsky loves her work and gives back generously, cheerfully, and with great enthusiasm. She is an official NFL Cheerleader of Life and in this role she has spoken to NFL program participants about the importance of education. She talks about her career and personal achievements. Sharing her experiences with children of all ages—the race car driver visits schools, hospitals, youth homes, and other organizations presenting a message to stay in school, eat and live right, stay off of drugs, set goals, and live your dream.

Zavodsky extends her faith through speaking events, pilgrimages, Bible study, and fellowship group. A cradle Catholic, she grew up in a strict religious home and went to Catholic schools. She prays before her races and says the Rosary on all commercial flights. She believes that Divine intervention and her Guardian Angel have kept her safe. Audrey Zavodsky was inducted into the Sports Faith International Hall of Fame in 2012.

RUN TO FINISH

Therefore, since we are surrounded by so great a cloud of witnesses, let us also lay aside every weight, and sin which clings so closely, and let us run with perseverance the race that is set before us, looking to Jesus the pioneer and perfecter of our faith, who for the joy that was set before him endured the cross, despising the shame, and is seated at the right hand of the throne of God. Consider him who endured from sinners such hostility against himself, so that you may not grow weary or fainthearted.

— Hebrews 12:1-3,

Before you run to finish,
You have to start to run.
Take nothing for granted.
You might not even have fun.

Losing hard is very hard.
Just ask William Perry.

Once you are in motion.
Depression is behind you.

Through the forest gleaming,
Run with perseverance,
Not sackcloth and ashes.

While your strength is gleaning,
Be earnest for Jesus.
Finish and earn danish.

— Patrick McCaskey

BELMONT ABBEY COLLEGE WALKWAY

WSFI Radio

Pope Saint John Paul II, who was known as "the athlete's Pope," called for the aggressive use of the media to promote the faith and utilize sports as a powerful instrument to share the Gospel of Jesus Christ. I am Chairman of Sports Faith International, an initiative that sets out to answer the Pope's call. Sports Faith International has recognized athletes, coaches, and others who are successful in sports while leading exemplary lives. At a gathering each year, we present awards, celebrate accomplishment, and thank God for His gifts. On December 9, 2013, we also launched WSFI Catholic Radio that broadcasts to listeners in northern Illinois and southern Wisconsin. WSFI offers Catholic Christian programing that promotes the faith.

In these initiatives, we do good works quietly, for God's glory. We fear God and we respect both our supporters and opponents. We work diligently and we trust God for the results. We go forward in faith.

We are especially grateful for the following: God created a wonderful world in six days; Jesus died for our sins, including mistakes; and when we need the Holy Spirit, He is present. He is even present when we think that we don't need Him.

We are hopeful that the world will not end until WSFI has paid off its bank loans. We want to do our programming with cooperation that is like an Amish barn-raising. We go to Mass and Bible study and have daily devotions. Our mandate is to love God and each other. And in our attempts to love, we are often funny. We have no soloists, we praise God as a full choir. We are thankful for our gifts and grateful for the opportunities that come our way. Sports Faith International and WSFI are reminders that God performs miracles for people of faith who diligently work together.

J.P. McCASKEY

SERVE THE LORD

*And if you be unwilling to serve the LORD, choose
this day whom you will serve, whether the gods your
fathers served in the region beyond the River, or the
gods of the Amorites in whose land you dwell; but as
for me and my house, we will serve the LORD.*

— Joshua 24:15

My grandfather George Halas's family came from
Bohemia. Many people know his story—how he
worked with other men to establish the NFL and
how he coached and owned the Chicago Bears. But my father's family made their mark as well.

CAST OF MCCASKEYS

We often joke that my father's ancestors, the McCaskeys,
were thrown out of Scotland for stealing horses. However, my
father's side of the family has its share of great Americans—
those who stepped out to serve the greater community. One of
the most remarkable McCaskeys was John Piersol McCaskey.
Although he lived over 150 years ago, he is still remembered
in his home town of Lancaster, Pennsylvania. They can't forget him—they named the high school after him.

John Piersol McCaskey

Early Americans often had a sense of duty to contribute to their community. The McCaskeys arrived at the birth of our nation. John McCaskey emigrated from Inverness in 1790. He had a son named William. William's wife, Marget, loved to sing. The family's most important book was the Bible.

Their oldest child, John Piersol (J.P.) McCaskey, was born October 9, 1837. Like his mother, J.P. was fond of music. In May 1849, he moved from Gordonville, Pennsylvania, with his family to Lancaster, Pennsylvania. He graduated from Boys High School in 1855. As a young teacher there, he fell in love with another teacher, Ellen Chase, who was born March 3, 1837 in Bath, New York. Ellen accepted J.P.'s marriage proposal via letter. They were married August 8, 1860 in Bath.

Two mules pulled their canal boat to Albany, New York, for their honeymoon. J.P. was wearing a plug hat that she didn't like. So he threw it into the canal. After their honeymoon, they returned to Lancaster.

J.P. served as principal of the high school from 1865 to 1906. He had learned the printing business by first offering to work without pay. From 1866 to 1921, he was a co-editor of the Pennsylvania School Journal. In 1867 he wrote the Christmas song, "Jolly Old Saint Nicholas." The "Johnny who wants a pair of skates" in the song was a son who died quite young.

J.P. spent Monday through Friday in the classroom. When boys misbehaved in class, he called upon them to hit each other's hands with a heavy ruler. He did not hit them himself. On Saturdays, he went to Philadelphia and New York for concerts and lectures. One winter he went to Niagara Falls to see it frozen. He knew the stars and constellations as God's marvelous handiwork.

He received a Master of Arts and a Doctorate of Philosophy from Franklin and Marshall College in Lancaster. In 1887 he began editing eight volumes of songs and ballads for Harper Brothers. In 1891 he published "Christmas in Song, Sketch, and Story." In 1897 he published the "Lincoln Literary Collection" which had extensive prose, poetry, and Biblical quotations. In 1899 he published "Favorite Songs and Hymns." In 1916 he also published three hardbound volumes entitled "Treasury of Song."

To each graduate of the school he gave a portrait of himself with this inscription: "The best of men that ever wore earth about him was a patient sufferer, a soft meek, tranquil Spirit, the first true gentleman that ever breathed." It was a quote by writer Thomas Dekker about Jesus.

Here are some quotes from J.P.'s writings.

"To assume that ability to spell, naming the letters of a word in their appointed order; to read, calling words at sight, often with little apprehension of the thought; to cipher, with fair degree of accuracy in mechanical results – these things are 'education!' and here to pause, is to be content with a very low standard of attainment. It is to live in the sub-cellar of a palace, when you might command, if you so desired, a broad

outlook from spacious windows higher up in the free air of heaven, under the stars.

"...the older I grow the more I appreciate the value of a thorough college or university course of study. Tens of thousands in money would weigh little with me now against an early four years course under the good men of Franklin and Marshall College, and a postgraduate course in some great university. I did not and could not have it.

"...Since high school, I have taken all the good of every sort – fun and earnest, if you like – that I have been able to get. My university has been the book, the newspaper, the play, the concert, the opera, the lecture, the sermon, the church, the world of nature, the world of art, the printing office, the dictionary, the cyclopedia, the poem, the restraining influence of the school, the blessed association of friends. Time and money have been of value only as they could be changed into what I wanted more. I have spent thousands of dollars in the past thirty years to see and hear the best in art and music in Philadelphia and elsewhere....I have to be in touch intellectually and spiritually with the best souls of the present and the past, with their strength and their goodness – souls 'forever young.'

"Education runs out on so many lines! It has to do with nature and art and life and the things of Time and

*the dream of Eternity. It takes in acquaintance with
books, but no less the butterfly and the bird, the grass
and the flower, the leaf and the habit of the tree, the
billowy wheat, the rustling corn, the wind and cloud,
air and earth, and sea and sky, with their myriad wonders of animate and inanimate creation; music, with its
melody and harmony; gratitude to our fellows for the
many good things in which we should hold ourselves
their debtors; and to God, 'in whom we live and move
and have our being.'"*

*"Wonder! at what? What not, indeed? Wonder at
everything! nor be fools enough to think we have
reached time or place when it is unbecoming. 'Angels
adore and wonder.' Foolish men do neither."*

In 1906 he gave up his high school work to become the
Republican Mayor of Lancaster. He served two 2-year terms.
His election was not much of a race—he walked into the
mayor's office because everybody who ever went to the high
school carried a big coin with his picture. The inscription was
"I am one of Jack's boys."

When he retired, he said:

*"Nothing is left but our work. And that is worth leav-
ing only as it is worthy.*

*"...The worthy person must always be a person good
to live with. The stronger, the truer, the more generous,*

the more courageous, the more energetic, the more enthusiastic, the more loving, the more noble – all the fine adjectives – the more wholesome is his influence."

On his ninetieth birthday, he said,

"Today I begin my ninetieth year; I have never thought much of dying. I have never believed much in it. Life has been so real, so natural, so good, and I have always been young."

Dick McCaskey

When my father was a young man, his family lived at 304 West King Street in a lovely old home right on the corner of West King and Mulberry; a corner that became occupied by a gas station. The McCaskeys were struggling in a deep depression and to survive, families consolidated. As a result, his sisters and brothers and he lived with his mother, his father, his grandfather, and his great grandfather.

Dick McCaskey was an interesting man who fought desperately with unemployment for many years, as did most of the men of Lancaster and, in fact, of all America. His grandfather was a retired Army officer, who had graduated from West Point with General Pershing. Thanks to his Army retirement check, they all managed to eat.

On April 20, 1959, I received the Sacrament of Confirmation. My grandfather, Dick McCaskey, was my sponsor. He was a genius with things electrical and mechanical. He could fix anything. He taught me how to fix a flat bike tire. He built a shower in our basement, wooden sidings to our laundry tubs, cabinets and closets, a brick sandbox attached to our garage, a swing set, and a dog pen.

My grandfather also taught me how to play catcher. He said that after a batter swung and missed a pitch I should show the batter the ball and say to him, "This is it, this little old round thing. This is what you're trying to hit." When I was watching a football game on television one day, he said, "They ought to give each team a ball. Then they wouldn't fight over it."

When my brothers and sisters and I came home from grammar school, our first question was "Where's Mom?" My grandfather tried to protect my mother and said, "Leave your mother alone. She's taking a well deserved nap." When that response didn't work, he said, "She went down to the Phila-delphia Naval Yard to dedicate a ship."

My mother gave crew cuts to my brothers and me. Then my grandfather would rub our heads and say, "I like the way you comb your hair." My grandfather liked to have cold milk at dinner. So he was the last one to have his milk poured. Some-times we forgot. Then he would hold his glass up to the light and say, "I wonder what I'm supposed to do with this. I guess I'll use it to look at stars tonight."

When my grandfather was visiting us in Des Plaines, Illi-nois, he often wrote to my grandmother, Kit McCaskey, in Lan-caster, Pennsylvania. The mailbox was a half a block away. He took turns saying to his grandchildren, "If you can mail this and get back here in two minutes, I'll give you a quarter." Regardless of how quickly each of us delivered the mail and ran back to him, he looked at his watch and said, "You just missed."

At dinner one evening when I was about ten, I did an impersonation of my grandfather impersonating Groucho Marx. I said, "After dinner, I think I'll play with my tool kit."

Jim McCaskey

My uncle Jim McCaskey was born on June 1, 1929. He unveiled the portrait of J. P. McCaskey when the new John Piersol McCaskey High School was completed and dedicated on May 3, 1938 in Lancaster, Pennsylvania. Jim McCaskey played end for the McCaskey High School football team. He edited the McCaskey High School newspaper.

Jim McCaskey graduated from the University of Pennsylvania as an English major. He served in the United States Army and kept the North Koreans above the 38th parallel. Jim McCaskey married Margaret Thompson in 1956 and kept a low profile so as not to take attention away from the wedding of Grace Kelly and Prince Ranier in 1956. He taught me to say "All that I am, all that I hope to be is because of my Uncle Jim."

Jim McCaskey was a great and valued letter writer. One time, when I drove his mother, Kit McCaskey, from Lancaster to his home in Paoli, before she got out of the car, he said to her, "Now Mother, don't start leaving. You just got here." Another time, right before the kickoff of a Bears' game in Philadelphia, Jim said to his brother, Tom, "Tom, if we leave now, we can beat the traffic." When you are sleeping, rapid eye movements are good for you. One night, before his wife, Maggie, went to bed, he said to her, "May you have rapid eye movements."

For my 33rd birthday, my uncle Jim gave me permission to date. My first date was with Gretchen at my parents' 40th anniversary party. Now we have three sons: Ed, Tom, and James. They were named after my father and his brothers in the same birth order.

Edward McCaskey

Catholic High School in Lancaster, Pennsylvania presented my father with an alumni citation award after he had died. It was an august occasion. I'm Catholic so I have a lot of relatives. Some of them were there that night: my mother, Aunt Betty, Aunt Kay, Uncle Jim, Aunt Maggie, Aunt Maggie's sister Kay, Cousin Kevin, his wife Susan, their children Claire and Libby, Cousin Kelly, Cousin Joe and his wife Ginny.

My father had given me a letter that I shared with the audience. It's the football letter that he earned at Catholic High. His brother, Tom, and his nephews Phil and Kevin were also great athletes at Catholic High. Saint Mary's School and Catholic High helped to form my father as a good Catholic, husband, brother, father, uncle, and grandfather. My father said that receiving a diploma from Lancaster Catholic High School was one of the most important things that happened in his life. He learned to think and to utilize the talents that God gave him. He continued to expand and enjoy all that life has to offer.

For the first six years of my parents' marriage, I was not here. I only know the legend. Three wise men from the East—Bert Bell, Bill Lennox, and Art Rooney[82]—followed a bright star until they found my father at the University of Pennsylvania Theater. They approved of him, much to the despair of Chief Papa Bear.

My mother's Indian name was Laughing Girl. My father put my mother on a donkey and they fled to Baltimore and they got married. In lieu of money, they gave the donkey to the priest. More than 10 months after the wedding my brother Mike was born in Pennsylvania. He was wrapped in an army blanket and laid in an open footlocker.

Across the Atlantic Ocean, Hitler had captured much of Europe. My father had heard that Hitler's ultimate goal was the capture of Ireland. So my father with his friend Max Kendrick and a sling and five smooth stones defeated Hitler. Later when Brian Piccolo had to go to New York City for cancer treatments, his wife, Joy, stayed at the Manhattan apartment of Max and Dorothy Kendrick.

Another friend who became an actor, Phil Foster, was also very helpful. Foster went on to play Frank De Fazio on Laverne and Shirley among many other roles. Phil Foster said that my father was the world's greatest unknown singer.

Upon my father's return to Pennsylvania, he met my brother Tim, who cried and cried at the introduction. My sister Ellen was also born there. When my mother was pregnant with me, the family moved to Illinois. Mary, Ned, Anne, George, Rich, Brian, and Joseph were also born here.

My brother George came along a little late. Max Kendrick, had said to my father, "Ed, all of your troubles with your father-in-law will be over if you just name your next son after him."

My father replied, "Nothing doing." Shortly after my birth, my father sent Kendrick a small baby trophy with the name Patrick Kendrick McCaskey. My father was so stubborn that he named the next son after himself: Edward William McCaskey. Finally, the next son was named George Halas McCaskey.[83] That was in 1956 and the Bears began their quest for a new stadium.

My parents have had the most influence on my spiritual development. They sacrificed to send their 11 children to parochial grade schools and high schools. Some went to Catholic colleges and universities. My family prayed together and worked together. During Lent, we prayed the rosary out loud together on our knees in the living room. When we misbehaved, we were strongly reminded, "This is the family rosary!"

I wanted to get married when I was in eighth grade because my parents had a great marriage. That was in 1963. My parents' marriage was in its 20th orbit. Sheila Quinn said that I should dance with other girls.

It's wonderful that all of us are here. Each of us was my father's favorite.

In 2012, Matthew Kelly published a book entitled "The Four Signs of a Dynamic Catholic." What would my father, Ed McCaskey, say about this book? I think he would say, "It's about me."

Once, my father looked at my wife's cross stitching of the fruits of the Holy Spirit. They are love, joy, peace, patience, longsuffering, gentleness, goodness, faith, meekness, temperance. My father said, "There's a list of all my qualities."

The four signs of a dynamic Catholic are prayer, study, generosity, and evangelization.

My father was a man of prayer. He went to Mass every day. He said the rosary every day. He used to say, "In your prayers, remember the Bears." My father believed that if you sing, you pray twice. He sang more than once. He double prayed quite often. My father was a man who studied. He read a lot of books. He went on a yearly retreat to Manresa in New Orleans.[84]

When he was a lector, he used to say, "You better get there early. There's usually a big crowd when I'm the lector." There used to be wallet cards that read, "I am a Catholic. In case of an accident, please call a priest." My father had a wallet card that read, "I am an important Catholic. In case of an accident, please call a bishop."

My father was a very generous man even though he said that fundraising was "Let's do great things with your money." At the first Notre Dame High School Dinner Auction, there was a raffle. The first prize was $10,000. Before the winning ticket had been drawn, my father walked forward as if he were the winner. He had bought so many tickets, he was the winner. Then he let the school keep the money.

My father evangelized. He used to say and write, "Keep the faith." After my father would have a speaking engagement someone would ask him how he did. My father would reply, "I was sensational." At my parents' fifty-fifth anniversary dinner party for several hundred people, he got up and said, "I don't care if you're Catholic or Protestant or Jewish. Everyone here ought to go to Mass every day."

Gardening Parables

Working in the garden had a special significance for my father— it became important to us as well. And just as weeds would come up and need attention in the garden, my father was always looking after us and the things that influenced our lives and character. He never gave up on his children and he never tired of encouraging us.

Irish poet Seamus Heaney wrote this about his father in the garden:

> So I saw him
> Down on his hands and knees beside the leek rig,
> Touching, inspecting, separating one
> Stalk from the other, gently pulling up
> Everything not tapered, frail and leafless,
> Pleased to feel each little weed-root break.[85]

Gardening parables remind me of a story that I use in my presentations that often gets a good response from football fans. In 1966, I went to the Bears Camp at St. Joseph's College in Rensselaer, Indiana, with my brother George, my brother Ned, and a high school football teammate, Ken Powers. At the start of our visit, my grandfather called us over to his golf cart after practice. He gave us some pocket money. When tight end Mike Ditka observed the transaction he came over to participate. He said, "Hey coach how about some of that for me?" My grandfather replied, "Never mind." Papa Bear's favorite parable was the one about the workers in the vineyard.

THANKS TO ED MCCASKEY

My father obeyed the law of gravity. He considered it a privilege to help his father in the garden. He never talked back to his mother.

He defeated the Nazis in World War II. He captured Mount Saint Jean.

He chose our mother. He renounced Satan and all his works and all his empty promises.

My father attended many, many, many Fathers Club meetings. He encouraged us to forsake alcohol. He encouraged our teachers to keep trying.

He said, "I can't do everything."

He said, "In your prayers, remember the Bears."

On April 30, 1957, he took us out of school to see the movie "Around the World in 80 Days" at the Michael Todd Theater in Chicago.

He helped us by doing interviews and making appearances. He "always tried to be a good husband and father."

He said, "The 80th division only moves forward."

He taught us the value of education. He instilled in us an appreciation of flowers. He taught us the importance of tying plastic bags into knots so that the kids at the garbage dumps wouldn't suffocate themselves.

He always kept a song in his heart which he passed on

to us. He took us fishing. He put smiley faces on our report cards. He took us to the Sugar Bowl Restaurant.

He sang in public. He built fires in the fireplace. He built bridges among family members. He allowed his sons to steal his clothes. He was the most decent human being in the National Football League.

He let us wheelbarrow truckloads of stone, sand, and good black earth. He led us in the rosary. He made sure we always had a dog.

He took his daughters to the Pump Room for Easter.

He made sure that each of us got a book for Christmas. He took us to Maryville on Christmas Day and he did not leave us there.

He taught us that ending a sentence in a preposition was unheard of. He taught us how to behave during Mass. He taught us it's important to have a good garden and someone else to work in it.

He showed us how to run a family like the Army. He let us wish him a happy birthday because presents were too expensive.

My father reminded us that God said, "Honor your father and your mother."

— Patrick McCaskey

Ed McCaskey, died on Tuesday, April 8, 2003. That Saturday, his funeral took place at Maryville Academy in Des Plaines. My father was a distinguished person. Thank you very much to my mother, my brothers and sisters, the Bears' trainers, my father's doctors and nurses, and all of you for taking great care of my father.

O son, help your father in his old age, and do not grieve him as long as he lives; even if he is lacking in understanding, show forbearance; in all your strength do not despise him. For kindness to a father will not be forgotten, and against your sins it will be credited to you;
— *Sirach 3:12-14,*

FULLNESS OF STRENGTH
When Peter and John arrived
At the Tomb,
John let Peter enter first
Because
He was the elder.
John had run
And
Peter might have told John that
He should do some stretching
Before entering.
When you are spiritually attuned,
God gives you the strength

To be obedient to His will.
When you are no longer living
In your parents' home
And
Your father asks you
To help him
With the gardening,
Remember:
Only a fool forgets his roots.

— Patrick McCaskey

Tribute to Virginia McCaskey

On January 5, 1923, my mother, Virginia Marion Anne Halas McCaskey, was born in Chicago. On February 13, 1923, she received the Sacrament of Baptism at Saint Mel's Church. Her grandmother, Barbara Halas, and her uncle, Walter Halas, were her godparents. On May 13, 1934, she made her First Communion at Saint Hilary's Church.

After she had graduated from Saint Scholastica Academy, she went off to the Drexel Institute of Technology in Philadelphia. She studied business because she wanted to be her father's secretary. Then she met my father on a semi-blind date.

On February 2, 1943, my parents received the Sacrament of Matrimony at Saint Margaret's Church in Bel Air, Maryland. On October 21, 1947, my mother received the Sacrament of

Confirmation at Saint Mary's Church in Manhasset, New York. She was married with three children: Mike, Tim, and Ellen. As a soldier of Christ, she was prepared for the next eight children: Mary, Ned, Anne, George, Rich, Brian, Joseph, and me.

My mother always found it amusing when someone asked her how much hired help she had. That was probably the reason my father nicknamed her Laughing Girl. She did all the cooking and laundry and housework. The only real time she got a break was when she went into the hospital to have another baby.

Our version of family planning was to have the children born during the Chicago Bears' off-seasons. We had seven victories and four ties.

My mother is my hero because she accepts God's grace and mercy and forgives those who trespass against her. She lives the gospel. Mom spelled upside down is "WOW."

Wonderful mother, thank you for life,
I am even grateful when there is strife;
Each of my cells has twenty-three
of your chromosomes how lucky for me!
Wonderful mother, here is a song,
It's the least I can do so says my wife;
Here are the Bears in life's busy throng
Wonderful mother, oh thank you for life!
Wonderful mother, oh thank you for life!

— Patrick McCaskey

THINK ABOUT THESE THINGS

...whatever is true,
whatever is honorable,
whatever is just,
whatever is pure,
whatever is lovely,
whatever is gracious,
if there is any excellence
and if there is anything worthy of praise,
think about these things.

— Philippians 4:8

When it comes to making a living in an entirely new field, you need faith to get started and you have to maintain faith as well. With faith, good things are always down the road.

BIDWILL'S CARDINALS

Of the original 11 professional football teams that made up the National Football League, only two survived: the Bears and the Cardinals. Many teams folded, especially in the early days of football.

Before NFL teams were on solid footing, the Great Depression set in. The economy improved and World War II came about. After the war, a new competitive league was established. In the 90+ years since the NFL's founding, the Bears moved from Decatur where they were called the Staleys to Chicago where they became the Bears. Originally called the Racine Cardinals because most of the team's players came from Chicago's south side around Racine Avenue, the Cardinals moved from Chicago to St. Louis and then on to Arizona.

Football's Dream Team

In 1932, the Cardinals were purchased by Charles Bidwill, a prominent Chicago attorney and sports figure. Bidwill's family was a spirited one with great energy and ambition. Bidwill was Jesuit educated at Saint Ignatius College Prep and Loyola University. He was a great football fan who had an ownership interest in the Bears before his Cardinal purchase. He had a great enthusiasm for sports and according to Bob Braunwart and Bob Carroll:

> *he was a winner, and he determined that his team would be the same.*[86]

After struggling to keep his Cardinals running through the Depression and World War II, Bidwill signed All-American Charley Trippi of Georgia, to a $100,000 contract. Bidwill had been busy making key draft choices during the lean war years and with his latest acquisition he had assembled the "Dream Backfield" of Paul Christman, Pat Harder, Marshall "Biggie" Goldberg, and Trippi. Coach Jimmy Conzelman added Elmer Angsman to the backfield mix and used Biggie

Goldberg as a defensive back. The Cardinals flew to the NFL championship in 1947. Sadly, Charles Bidwill had died from pneumonia that spring. Bidwill had helped solidify the league when he bought the Cardinals and he was enshrined in the Pro Football Hall of Fame as a member of the class of 1967.

Following Charles death, his wife, Violet, led the franchise followed jointly by sons William (Bill) and Charles, Jr. (Stormy). Bill became sole owner in 1972 while Stormy moved into other family interests.

William V. Bidwill's association with the Cardinals football team began when he served as his dad's ball boy on Chicago's South Side where the Cardinals played. Bidwill has seven decades of involvement with the team.

Bidwill attended Georgetown University and served in the Navy. After the service, he returned to his family's businesses in Chicago. The owners moved the Cardinals to St. Louis in 1960. Following the 1997 season, the Cardinals moved to Arizona. In August of 2006, the team opened the state-of-the-art University of Phoenix Stadium, which gave the franchise a true home of its own. All home games at the new stadium have been sold out.

An active supporter of various civic and charitable organizations, Bidwill directed the formation of Cardinals' Charities, the team's organization dedicated to supporting worthy Arizona causes.

One of Bidwill's charities is Saint Peter Mission School. Seven Franciscan Sisters of Christian Charity serve at the school living among the Gila River Community. School Principal Sister Martha Mary Carpenter has spent her life working with underprivileged Native American children. Her students learn native language, custom, and art at the school in addition to their other subjects. The community suffers from gangs, drugs, crime, but the school is safe and welcoming.

Bidwill avoids publicity surrounding his generosity, but some notice is unavoidable. Sister Martha has thanked him for his support and she jokes:

> *"He teases me whenever I call. He says, 'Now what do you want?'"*

Bidwill is co-chair of the Board of Trustees for the Bert Bell/Pete Rozelle Player Benefit Plan and he serves on the Board of Trustees for the Pro Football Hall of Fame. Bidwill and his wife, Nancy, are the parents of five children and have nine grandchildren. Bill and Nancy's son Michael, an attorney, now serves as President of the Arizona Cardinals.

WILLETT HANDS OFF TO CASEY WHO TOSSES THE BALL TO HENNESSEY FOR THE SCORE

My family has had a long association with Notre Dame Prep in Niles, Illinois. In my 50 plus year association with the great school, I have a deep appreciation of the great sacrifices and hard work coaches, teachers, and administrators put into their work.

Fran "the Silver Fox" Willett was born April 27, 1924 in Milwaukee, Wisconsin, and raised in Hannibal, Missouri, the hometown of Mark Twain. Willett played football, basketball, and baseball at McCooey High School where he met his wife, Mary. The Willetts had seven children: Michael, Patrick, Kathleen, Timothy, Thomas, Terrence, and Carolyn.

Willett served 3 1/2 years with the Fourth Marine Division. He had three years in the Pacific during World War II which we won. Then he went to Northeast Missouri State on the GI Bill and an athletic scholarship. He played football, basketball, and baseball there.

Willett coached for 15 years before he arrived at Notre Dame High School in September, 1964. I was a sophomore and during my lunch breaks, Coach Willett explained the option series and the counter play. The power sweep was used to entertain the fans and the players. Seven players would come around the end. There was certainly little need to throw a pass.

Each day during the summer of 1966 before my senior football season, I threw 200 passes and ran five miles. At the start of the three-a-day August drills, I won the football players' 600-yard run in 1:21.8. Coach Willett rewarded me; I was a linebacker.

In practice, I did well in the passing drills. Then I pouted when I did not get the opportunity to quarterback the first team. Coach Willett called me into his office. "Do you think you're the best quarterback we have?" he asked.

I replied, "Yes." Eventually, he let me play quarterback too.

We finished 9–0 and outscored opponents 341–80. There were no playoffs then. In 1982, Fran Willett was inducted into the Illinois High School Football Coaches Hall of Fame. In 46 years of coaching, he had 90 teams. I am very grateful that I had the opportunity of playing on one of them. He helped me grow up. He died in 1995.

Casey Takes the Handoff

Bill Casey was born in 1937 and grew up in Mansfield, Ohio, where he played several sports for Saint Peter's High School. At the University of Notre Dame, he played on the freshman baseball team, and graduated as a biology major. Casey agreed to teach and coach at Notre Dame High School for a year; he stayed for decades. Casey started his coaching career with the swimming team.

When I was a freshman at Notre Dame High School in 1963, Casey was the freshman football coach. When I was a sophomore, Casey was the sophomore football coach. When I was a junior, he was the offensive coordinator of the varsity football team. He also let me work out with the swimming team. When I was a senior, he was the offensive coordinator of the 1966 varsity football team that won every game by an average score of 38–9.

Casey succeeded Willett as varsity football coach and became athletic director. He held both jobs for a while, but he settled on AD where he oversaw 12 varsity sports. His job involved scheduling events, officials, transportation, and workers. He hired the head coaches.

Coach Casey liked seeing kids succeed. He knew they worked hard over a long period of time. Then he went to events and saw them succeed. Coach Casey helped many people and he received letters of appreciation. He read them during down times. He was also under the spotlight and he got criticized. He worked very hard. He wasn't in it for the money.

Coach Casey identified with John the Baptist who paved the way for Christ. As athletic director, he went ahead and prepared for the events. He heard about it when something went wrong. It was difficult to get money to support the school's programs. He became a fundraiser.   Because of him, we were able to have alumni track & field meets, alumni cross-country meets, and alumni intramural basketball tournaments. As much as anyone, he was responsible for a new track and the new parking lot. When I needed help to start the Chicago Bears Flag Football program for high school intramural athletes, he was the first person I called and he was very helpful. Coach Casey was a quiet leader. He died in 1994.

Hennessey Makes the Grab

Mike Hennessey attended a grade school with a great name: Our Lady of Victory. The school also has excellent colors: blue and orange.[87] Mike was class salutatorian at Gordon Tech High School; he was also captain and quarterback of the football team. Carl Sandburg played basketball for Lombard College. Lombard College became Knox College. Mike Hennessey played football for Knox College.

Mike was an assistant principal and eighth grade teacher at Saint Boniface Grade School. Then he was a history teacher, assistant recruitment director, and an assistant football coach for Gordon Tech. In 1980, they won the state championship. In 1985, Mike received a master's degree in Education and Administration from Northeastern Illinois University. In 1987, Mike became the football coach at what is now Notre Dame College Prep. He taught history for eight years. He also coached baseball. In 1995, he became the athletic director.

Mike has had much success as a football coach over 25 years. He's been the Notre Dame Father d'Autremont Faculty Member of the Year and the Niles Chamber of Commerce Coach of the Year. He is a member of the Illinois High School Football Coaches Association Hall of Fame, the Gordon Tech High School Hall of Fame, the East Suburban Catholic Conference Hall of Fame, and the Sports Faith International Hall of Fame.[88]

> *If you put these instructions before the brethren, you will be a good minister of Christ Jesus, nourished on the words of the faith and of the good doctrine which you have followed. Have nothing to do with godless and silly myths. Train yourself in godliness; for while bodily training is of some value, godliness is of value in every way, as it holds promise for the present life and also for the life to come.*
>
> — *1 Timothy 4:6-8*

MIKE McCOY

Mike McCoy is a native of Erie, Pennsylvania, and a graduate of Cathedral Prep High School. At Cathedral Prep, McCoy's coach Tony Zambrowski was a Notre Dame alum who introduced him to the school. At Notre Dame, McCoy was a three-year letter-winner and consensus All-American under former Irish coach Ara Parseghian.

At Notre Dame, McCoy recalled the fierce rivalries against USC and Michigan State. His best game was against USC where he managed to keep at least one Heisman Trophy winner in check.[89] During his senior year, Notre Dame lost a bowl game against the University of Texas who won the National Championship.

Unlike today's top draft picks, McCoy did not travel to New York for the draft although he was a top draft choice. In 1969, the Pittsburgh Steelers were 1–13. So were the Bears. There was a coin flip to determine who would have the first pick of the NFL Draft. The Bears lost the toss. The Steelers chose Terry Bradshaw. The Bears traded the pick to the Green Bay Packers. The Packers chose Mike McCoy.

McCoy played 11 seasons with the Packers, Oakland Raiders, and the New York Giants. McCoy was defensive tackle and he was named Packers Rookie of the Year in 1970. He led the Packers in quarterback sacks in 1973 and 1976. Among many other awards, he received the Bronko Nagurski Legends award, which recognized the top defensive players in the last 40 years.

Post NFL

Five years after his NFL career had ended, McCoy's grade school daughter gave her dad some ideas for a second career. She told him about the pressures and temptations she and other kids were feeling at school. McCoy decided to join NFL players around the country to speak at schools and serve as positive role models. McCoy later formed the Mike McCoy Ministries program. He used his Notre Dame and NFL background to reach people and spread his message. McCoy has a big job. He believes every student in America is at risk due to cultural influences that reduce the influence of family and faith.

Mike McCoy's passion is empowering youth and helping them develop a larger vision for their lives. He has a faith-based message of hope and encouragement.

FAITH BY EXAMPLE

GEORGE HALAS AND BILL WADE

I can do all things in him who strengthens me.

— Philippians 4:13

In sports there are many athletes who lead by example. It gives an author a lot to rely on for books like this. My grandfather was someone I looked up to and his example was powerful. In this final chapter I look at my grandfather and his thoughts.

PAPA BEAR'S THOUGHTS

In the summer of 1915, my grandfather, George Halas, worked for Western Electric in Chicago. On Saturday, July 24 the company was scheduled for a ride on a ship called the Eastland in the Chicago River. My grandfather missed the boat; it rolled over on its side and 844 people died. If he hadn't missed the boat, the National Football League, the Chicago Bears, and I might not be here. Sometimes it's okay to be late.

My grandfather lettered in football, basketball, and baseball at the University of Illinois. He graduated with a degree in engineering in 1918. After my grandfather had graduated from college, he was in the service at the Great Lakes Naval Station. He played sports for them too. He was the most valuable player in the 1919 Rose Bowl. You could look it up. He played right field for the 1919 New York Yankees and batted .091. Then he played for the 1919 Hammond Pros football team.

On March 18, 1920, George Chamberlain met with my grandfather in Chicago. Chamberlain was the general superintendent of the Staley Company in Decatur. Halas was working in the bridge department of the Chicago, Burlington, & Quincy Railroad.

Chamberlain offered Halas the opportunity to learn the starch business and be the company's athletic director and football coach. He could also play on the Staley football and baseball teams. Halas accepted. The sports headline in the March 19 *Decatur Review* read "George 'Chic' Hallas Joins Staley Forces."

In 1921, there was a recession. Mister Staley couldn't afford to finance the football team anymore. He gave my grandfather $5,000 to move the team to Chicago with the stipulation that the team nickname be the Staleys for one year. (My grandfather was up for a promotion in the glucose department.) So, in 1921, the team was the Chicago Staleys; they won the first of nine championships.

In the winter of 1922, the team name was changed to the Chicago Bears and it's been that way ever since. On February 18, my grandfather and my grandmother, Min, got married. Grandchildren of Mister Staley sometimes wonder what their lives would have been like if their grandfather had sold the company and kept the team.

My grandfather, George Halas, was an optimist. America needed optimists as it battled through the Depression and two wars during the 20th Century. Those who knew my grandfather would tell you that he lived life with a passion every day and seldom looked back. He was not a philosopher. He had no ambitions about writing his thoughts on organizations, competition, and winning that might be used in business textbooks. His focus was always on football. His books were on the modified T formation and his life in football. But he did have a gift for providing support and encouragement. You will find Halas quotes spread out in books and on the Internet. Here are some of my favorites along with my thoughts on them.[90]

*"Don't do anything in practice that you wouldn't
do in the game."*

Halas came from a family that believed in hard work. He had no interest is wasting time because he believed there was no time for it. If you were wasting time, you were taking away time that you needed to apply elsewhere. And when he brought his team together, he wanted no wasted motions. When you waste time in practice, you waste it for everyone present.

> *"Find out what the other team wants to do.*
> *Then take it away from them."*

In competition of any kind, an opponent sets out to defeat you. And according to Halas, the best way to defeat competition is to stop them from doing what they want. If your opposition likes to run, you stop their running game. If they like to pass, you stop their passing game. If they win by taking advantage of your mistakes, you cut out the mistakes.

> *"Many people flounder about in life because they do not*
> *have a purpose, an objective toward which to work."*

A good coach likes to stick with a game plan, but the best coaches like to win. The best coaches have goals and they move forward from there. When Halas started out as the manager and coach of the Staleys, his objective was to build the best team. When the Staleys were turned over to Halas, his objective was to make the Staleys a success financially and on the field. When Halas found himself at the center of a new professional football league, his objective was to make the new league a success. He was building a team, developing a winning program, and establishing a viable league—all at once.

Halas was fierce after a loss—his wrath was legendary, but it lasted for a short time. Regardless of a game's outcome, Halas put it behind him and started thinking about next week's opponent.

"If you live long enough, lots of nice things happen."

George Halas took very good care of himself in terms of diet and exercise. Good goals and hard work led to success, but he also believed it was important to live long to see the success! Like many former football players, Halas had his share of wounds, some of which would dog him for the rest of his life, but he set out to do his best to maintain his health in ways that he could. While much of the world was still thinking retirement at age 65, Halas was coaching into his 70s and he managed the club well into his 80s.

"Nobody who ever gave his best regretted it."

In sports, it is common knowledge that the best teams are highly principled and the best coaches are hard to please. Great effort makes the most sense after the performance, after the win. Regret comes with falling short, but satisfaction comes with optimum effort.

"Nothing is work unless you'd rather be doing something else."

The most satisfying efforts are those that we take on without regret. The hungry athlete takes on exercise, study, training, and repetition with satisfaction knowing that it is leading to goals and objectives. If an athlete no longer shares his or her team's goals and aspirations, training becomes work. The athlete must overcome his opponents, but the most difficult thing to overcome is one's own misgivings. At some point in an athlete's career, it is time to move on.

"Never go to bed a loser."

We have all heard that to have a good marriage we should never go to bed angry. We should never leave any unresolved issues haunting us at night if possible. Halas took this advice a step further. We should never go to bed without having done what we can to make our lives successful and feeling like a success. We all lose at times, but a loser is someone with a damaged ego, who believe themselves to be a loser. Halas would say that you should never accept those kind of self-doubts. Do your best and believe that you are a winner and you will be one.

LOSING AND WINNING[91]

When your football team has a losing season,
Gossip is a replacement for reason.
Priests and ministers seem to pray in vain.
When your team loses, you are in disdain.
You wish your team were always in the hunt,
Featured like teams who never have to punt.
Your team has players who work together
And fans who are much more than fair weather.

Yet a gameless January gives you time
To wipe from your team defeat causing slime.
No time to settle into winter weight.
Work out. Help others. Don't hibernate.
　For victory is why your team competes.
　Wins are your team's most enjoyable treats.

— Patrick McCaskey

— ENDNOTES —

1. Both Washington Community High School and the Springfield Sacred Heart Griffin High School have been inducted into the Sports Faith International Hall of Fame. The Sports Faith International Hall of Fame recognizes athletes, coaches, and administrators in sports who lead exemplary lives. Schools are recognized for their like-kind accomplishments.

2. Father Theodore Hesburgh served as president of the University of Notre Dame from 1952-1989.

3. The College Championship was not officially designated by a single organization although most of the authorities named Notre Dame in 1973. What is called the coaches poll, published at the time by UPI, voted Alabama, but that vote was made before the Sugar Bowl defeat. Such controversy has historically surrounded the college football "championship."

4. "Dave Casper To Be Enshrined In The National Football Foundation College Football Hall of Fame," Notre Dame Fighting Irish Athletics home page, August 5, 2013, viewed at http://www.und.com/sports/m-footbl/spec-rel/080513aae.html on July 14, 2014.

5. Howie Long and John Czarnecki, *Football for Dummies* (New York: John Wiley, 2011) 355.

6. Nickname based on "Casper the Friendly Ghost."

7. The sun and the moon were symbols for Joseph's parents. Jacob responded to the dream by asking "Will your mother and I and your brothers actually come and bow down to the ground before you?"

8. Severin and Stephen Lamping (translation, arrangement, and foreword), *Through Hundred Gates: By Noted Converts from Twenty-Two Lands* (Milwaukee: Bruce Publishing Company, 1939) 41-42.

9. Maryville Academy has offered protection and guidance to children in need for more than 130 years. Its main facility is located in Des Plaines, Illinois.

10. Charlestown has since gentrified to where a single floor of an old frame house in Long's old neighborhood now serves as a condominium unit that often sells for well over half a million dollars.

11. Paul Zimmerman, "The Long Way Up," *Sports Illustrated Vault*, July 22, 1985, viewed at http://www.si.com/vault/1985/07/22/620587/the-long-way-up on July 10, 2014.

12. The Raiders moved from Oakland to Los Angeles before the 1982 season and they remained the Los Angeles Raiders for the remainder of Long's career.

13. Long shares his sentiments on football in *Football for Dummies* co-authored with fellow FOX associate, John Czarnecki and published over several editions by John Wiley.

14. Paul Zimmerman, "The Long Way Up," Sports Illustrated Vault, July 22, 1985, viewed at http://www.si.com/vault/1985/07/22/620587/the-long-way-up on July 10, 2014.

15. Jeff Greenfield, *The World's Greatest Team: A Portrait of the Boston Celtics from 1957-1969* (New York: Random House, 1976) 40.

16. Jamie Moyer and Larry Platt, *Just Tell Me I Can't* (New York: Grand Central Publishing, 2013) 6.

17. Surgery named after a pitcher Tommy John who received it and prolonged his career. The procedure reconstructs the ulnar collateral ligament in the medial elbow with a tendon. First performed in 1974 by orthopedic surgeon Dr. Frank Jobe.

18. Web site for "One Last Hug" viewed on September 11, 2014 at http://www.hbo.com/#/documentaries/one-last-hug-three-days-at-grief-camp.

19. Hunt was American Football League founder and his Dallas Texans/Kansas City Chiefs team and other AFL teams merged with the NFL.

20. Comedy directed by Mel Brooks.

21. Rick Hummel, "Musial Beyond Comparison," Saint Louis Post Dispatch, January 26, 2013 viewed at http://www.stltoday.com/sports/baseball/professional/rick-hummel-musial-beyond-comparison/article_22290e56-5df8-5c5e-9475-4169ccbc4386.html on March 6, 2013.

22. Ed Fitzgerald, *More Champions in Sports and Spirit* (New York: Vision Books, 1959) 16.

23. Jan Finkel, "Stan Musial," Society for American Baseball Research (SABR) biography viewed at http://sabr.org/bioproj/person/2142e2e5 on March 12, 2014.

24. For some years during Musial's career there were two All Star games.

25. George Vecsey, *Stan Musial* (New York: Ballantine Books, 2011) 208.

26. Joseph Kenny, "Baseball's Perfect Knight Was a Devout Catholic," Saint Louis Review, January 21, 2013. Viewed at http://stlouisreview.com/article/2013-01-21/baseball-s-perfect on March 12, 2014.

27. Joseph Kenny, "Baseball's Perfect Knight Was a Devout Catholic," Saint Louis Review, January 21, 2013. Viewed at http://stlouisreview.com/article/2013-01-21/baseball-s-perfect on March 12, 2014.

28. From Cardinal Dolan's "The Gospel in the Digital Age" Blog viewed at http://blog.archny.org/index.php/an-inspiration-to-generations/ on March 12, 2014.

29. Mimeograph is a low cost printing press used for making copies of documents before copying machines came into vogue. They are still in use in some places.

30. Tom Monaghan and Robert Anderson, *Pizza Tiger* (New York, Random House, 1986) 24-25.

31. Tom Monaghan and Robert Anderson, *Pizza Tiger* (New York, Random House, 1986), 339.
32. Monaghan's biography *Pizza Tiger* provides the interesting background and experiences of Tom Monaghan's life. See *Pizza Tiger* by Tom Monaghan with Robert Anderson published by Random House in 1986.
33. With thanks to Alfred Tennyson for "The Charge of the Light Brigade."
34. Coach Gordon's ministry was discussed in Sports and Faith Book 1 by Patrick McCaskey.
35. Matt McKinney, "Suburban Congregation Celebrates Life of Men Killed in Afghanistan Attack," Chicago Sun-Times.com, April 27, 2014, viewed at http://www.suntimes.com/news/metro/27090694-418/arlington-heights-congregation-celebrates-life-of-men-killed-in-afghanistan-attack.html#.U2JdDqIgzTQ on May 1, 2014.
36. The mother abbey of St. Michael's, the abbey of Csorna was resuscitated after the fall of Communism in the West.
37. History of St. Michael's Abbey of the Norbertine Fathers, viewed on June 10, 2014 at http://www.stmichaelsabbey.com/abbey/index.php?option=com_content&view=article&id=56&Itemid=65.
38. See the St. Michael's web site for the latest developments on the new abbey and other buildings that will support it: http://www.stmichaelsabbey.com/abbey/
39. Trent Beattie, "Ex-Baseball Phenom Discusses Life in a Norbertine Abbey," National Catholic Register, April 8, 2013, viewed on June 10, 2014 at http://www.ncregister.com/daily-news/ex-baseball-phenom-chose-the-better-part-in-norbertine-abbey/.
40. Father Joe Freedy's discernment is described in *Sports and Faith: Stories of the Devoted and the Devout*, Book I (2011) beginning on page 2. Freedy's image graces the cover of Book I as well.
41. Trent Beattie, "Ex-Baseball Phenom Discusses Life in a Norbertine Abbey," National Catholic Register, April 8, 2013, viewed on June 10, 2014 at http://www.ncregister.com/daily-news/ex-baseball-phenom-chose-the-better-part-in-norbertine-abbey/.
42. Trent Beattie, "Ex-Baseball Phenom Discusses Life in a Norbertine Abbey," National Catholic Register, April 8, 2013, viewed on June 10, 2014 at http://www.ncregister.com/daily-news/ex-baseball-phenom-chose-the-better-part-in-norbertine-abbey/.
43. Jeff Passan, "From Prospect to Priest: Grant Desme Leaves the A's, Becomes a Monk and Tries to Find His Peace," Yahoo Sports, September 27, 2012, viewed on June 10, 2014 at http://sports.yahoo.com/news/from-prospect-to-priest--grant-desme-leaves-the-a-s--becomes-a-monk-and-tries-to-find-his-peace.html .

44. Missionary Oblates of Mary Immaculate at http://www.oblatesusa.org/who-we-are/our-missionary-work/who-are-the-oblates/.

45. This amazing story is featured in a number of media outlets in recent years including "The Champions of Faith" DVD Series, a column by ESPN's Major League Baseball Analyst Tim Kurkjian and many more.

46. Amy Donnelly tombstone reads "The chicken runs at midnight."

47. McQuaid High School web site, viewed at http://www.mcquaid.org/page.cfm?p=9 on January 25, 2015.

48. Ken Kleppel, "From The Gridiron to The Supreme Court: Alan Page and Bob Thomas Still Making a Difference," Nov. 4, 2005, Notre Dame Fighting Irish Web Site, viewed at http://www.und.com/sports/m-footbl/spec-rel/110405aah.html on October 16, 2014.

49. Ken Kleppel, "From The Gridiron to The Supreme Court: Alan Page and Bob Thomas Still Making a Difference," Nov. 4, 2005, Notre Dame Fighting Irish Web Site, viewed at http://www.und.com/sports/m-footbl/spec-rel/110405aah.html on October 16, 2014.

50. Based on Henry the Fifth, Act III, Scene 1.

51. Most often, sources state that De La Salle was the national champion 6 times, but some sources list the Spartans as national champion 7 times.

52. "Strong of Heart," Profiles of Notre Dame Athletics 2013, viewed at http://frankallocco.com/strong-of-heart.pdf on January 12, 2015.

53. Mario Fraioli, "The Best Ever: Exclusive Interview with Jim Ryun," *competitor.com*, Nov. 29, 2010 viewed at http://running.competitor.com/2010/11/interviews/the-best-ever-exclusive-interview-with-jim-ryun_17818 on October 15, 2014.

54. "The List: Best High School Athletes Ever," *ESPN Page 2*, viewed at http://espn.go.com/page2/s/list/highschool.html on October 15, 2014.

55. Todd Anton and Bill Nowlin, *When Football Went to War* (Chicago: Triumph Books, 2013) 236.

56. Stephen Edelson, "Community Helped Family Heel After Loss of Son," *Asbury Park Press*, August 16, 2014, viewed at http://www.app.com/story/sports/high-school/football/2014/08/16/community-helped-duddy-family-heal-loss-son/14164203/ on February 20, 2015.

57. The quotes here are from Stephen Edelson's story on the loss of Francis Duddy. Readers are encouraged to read in the Asbury Park Press story at http://www.app.com/story/sports/high-school/football/2014/08/16/community-helped-duddy-family-heal-loss-son/14164203/.

58. Johnny Holliday and Stephen Moore, *Johnny Holliday: From Rock to Jock* (Champaign, IL, Sports Publishing LLC, 2002)157.

59. Peggy Schaefer Editor, *Guideposts for the Spirit: Stories of Changed Lives* (Nashville: Ideals Publishing, 2003) 191-195.

60. George Raine, "Catholic Athletes for Christ: Athletes of Faith Aim to Evangelize Sports World, Attack "Moral Crisis," Catholic San Francisco, August 25, 2010. Viewed at http://www.catholic-sf.org/news_select.php?newsid=23&id=57477 on March 5, 2014.

61. Pope Saint John Paul II, once an avid skier, swimmer, and hiker, established the Vatican Office of Church and Sport in 2004 on the eve of the Summer Olympic Games in Athens, a year before his death.

62. George Raine, "Catholic Athletes for Christ: Athletes of Faith Aim to Evangelize Sports World, Attack "Moral Crisis," *Catholic San Francisco*, August 25, 2010. Viewed at http://www.catholic-sf.org/news_select.php?newsid=23&id=57477 on March 5, 2014.

63. This material is adapted from Patrick McCaskey's *Pillars of the NFL: Coaches Who Have Won Three or More Games*, published by Sporting Chance Press in 2014.

64. Blue Springs Weekly Sentinel of May 15, 1913, reprinted in special anniversary booklet.

65. Wally Provost, "State College Set Must Have Cheered Chamberlin's Transfer to Husker," from Nebraska's Greatest Guy series, *Omaha World Herald*, August 26, 1964.

66. Official web site of the Chicago Bears, Tradition Page at http://www.chicagobears.com/tradition/bears-in-the-hall/paddy-driscoll.html

67. Chris Willis, "Ralph Hay, A Forgotten Pioneer," *The Coffin Corner*, Vol. 25 (2004).

68. Charlie Powell, "Colorful Show Climaxes Greatest Grid Weekend: HOF Adds 7 Notables to Shrine," *The Canton Repository*, Sept. 13, 1965.

69. Halas letter to Chamberlin's daughter, Mrs. Patricia Sherwood, on May 6, 1967, provided by Robert Sherwood, grandson of Guy Chamberlin.

70. ESPN Sports Century Feature viewed at https://espn.go.com/sportscentury/features/00014107.html on August 11, 2014.

71. ESPN Sports Century Feature viewed at https://espn.go.com/sportscentury/features/00014107.html on August 11, 2014. Kelly Boyer Sagert, Steven J. Overman, *Icons of Women's Sports* (Santa Barbara: Greenwood Press, 2012) 41.

72. Bonnie Blair signed copies of the February 2008 issue continue to sell online.

73. Bonnie Blair with Greg Brown, *A Winning Edge* (Dallas: Taylor Publishing, 1996) 40.

74. Amanda Hudson, "Fitness a Matter of Discipline for Bishop Malloy," *The Observer*, January 10, 2014, page 5.

75. Joseph Berger, "Another Step Up for the Bronx Native Who Led the Archdiocese in Baltimore," New York Times, January 6, 2012 viewed on July 2,

2014 at http://www.nytimes.com/2012/1/07/nyregion/es-baltimore-archbish-op-edwin-f-obrien-elevated-to-cardinal.html

76. See Stew Smith's web site for the story at http://www.stewsmith.com/link-pages/notquiteready.htm.

77. Lance Cpl. Andy Orozco, "New Priest Leads Catholic Services Aboard New River," Official Web Site of the United States Marines, viewed at http://www.newriver.marines.mil/News/NewsArticleDisplay/tabid/736/Article/149642/new-priest-leads-catholic-services-aboard-new-river.aspx on July 1, 2014.

78. Pope Pius XXII, Sports at the Service of the Spirit, July 29, 1945.

79. Lukas Johnson, "Belmont Abbey President Bill Thierfelder Discusses New Book, charlotteobserver.com, June 16, 2014 viewed at http://www.charlotteobserver.com/2014/06/16/4981706/belmont-abbey-president-bill-thierfelder.html#.U87OCrEadKI on July 22, 2014.

80. Kelly Conroy, "Reclaim the Game, Says Belmont Abbey College President," Catholic Education Daily, September 16, 2013, viewed at http://www.cardinalnewmansociety.org/CatholicEducationDaily/DetailsPage/tabid/102/ArticleID/2544/%E2%80%98Reclaim-the-Game-%E2%80%99-Says-Belmont-Abbey-College-President.aspx on July 22, 2014.

81. Kelly Conroy, "Reclaim the Game, Says Belmont Abbey College President," Catholic Education Daily, September 16, 2013, viewed at http://www.cardinalnewmansociety.org/CatholicEducationDaily/DetailsPage/tabid/102/ArticleID/2544/%E2%80%98Reclaim-the-Game-%E2%80%99-Says-Belmont-Abbey-College-President.aspx on July 22, 2014.

82. Modern readers may not know these men. Bell was the owner of the Philadelphia Eagles and became NFL Commissioner in 1946. Bill Lennox was the ticket manager for Franklin Field, the home of Pennsylvania and he knew McCaskey personally. Art Rooney was the owner of the Pittsburgh Steelers and a friend of Halas.

83. George Halas McCaskey is the current Chairman of the Chicago Bears Football Club.

84. Manresa House of Retreats, located in Convent, Louisiana, is recognized as one of the premier Jesuit retreat houses in the world.

85. Excerpt from "A Call" from OPENED GROUND: SELECTED POEMS 1966-1996 by Seamus Heaney. Copyright © 1998 by Seamus Heaney. Reprinted by permission of Farrar, Straus and Giroux, LLC.

86. Bob Braunwart and Bob Carroll, "Blue Shirt Charlie's Big Red Dream," The Coffin Corner, Vol 3, No. 4 (1981) viewed at https://www.profootball-researchers.org/Coffin_Corner/03-04-063.pdf on July 18, 2014.

87. Same as Chicago Bears colors.

88. Gordon Technical High School is now known as DePaul College Prep and has an academic partnership with DePaul University.
89. In 1968, McCoy's junior year, the Notre Dame defense held Heisman Trophy winner O.J. Simpson to a career-low 55 yards on 22 carries.
90. Quotes from famous people are sometimes found to be unoriginal. The author believes these are original, but the important point here is that these sayings represent George Halas's philosophy and the way he conducted his life.
91. With thanks to William Shakespeare for "Sonnet 29."

— Photographs and Illustrations Credits —

All photos and illustrations are produced with permission
(unless public domain) from the sources shown below.

Page	Description	Source
Cover	Burke Masters Celebration after Mississippi State University Victory	Mississippi State University
viii	Bob Ladouceur of De La Salle High School	Photo by Bob Sansoe of Sansoe Photography
1	Head Coach Darrell Crouch and Recent Team	Washington High School
2	Tornado Damage Washington, Illinois	National Weather Service
18	Knute Rockne	Library of Congress
27	Howie Long on Hangar Deck of the USS Harry S. Truman	DoD photo by Airman Apprentice Raynel Emmons, U.S. Navy
29	Bob Cousy	College of Holy Cross, Department of Athletics
39	Challenger Crew	NASA
43	Stan Musial	Missouri State Archives
49	Patrick McCaskey at Notre Dame College Prep Commencement, May 31, 2014	Notre Dame College Prep
54	Tom Monaghan, Tossing Pizza Dough	Ypsilanti Historical Society
55	Ave Maria University	Ave Maria University
72	Monk in Thought at St. Michael's Abbey of the Norbertine Fathers	Rick Belcher, Photographer
85	Burke Masters, SEC Scholar-Athlete of the Year	Mississippi State University
92	Michael Lightner as Student	Eastern Michigan University, Department of Athletics
94	Bill Dana and Danny Thomas	"The Danny Thomas Show," Public Domain Image
102	Bob Thomas	State of Illinois
110	Frank Allocco of De La Salle High School	Photo by Bob Sansoe of Sansoe Photography
116	Ron Meyer	Ron Meyer

225

127	Dan Duddy with Donovan Catholic High School Player	Donovan Catholic High School
140	Guy Chamberlin at Fort Kearney	Rob Sherwood, Grandson to Guy Chamberlin
164	Bishop Paprocki Blocks Shot Against St. Norbert	Diocese of Springfield, Chuck Cherney Photo
165	Bishop Malloy Visiting Prisoners and Saying Mass at Winnebago County Jail at Christmas	*Rockford Observer*
173	Bill Thierfelder	Belmont Abbey College
179	Belmont Abbey College Walkway	Belmont Abbey College
182	J.P. McCaskey photo	Courtesy of LancasterHistory.org, Lancaster, Pennsylvania.
211	George Halas and Bill Wade	*Chicago Tribune*

— INDEX —

— INDEX —